W0010609

SEX AND THE UNREAL CITY

*The Demolition of the Western Mind*

ANTHONY ESOLEN

# Sex and the Unreal City

## *The Demolition of the Western Mind*

IGNATIUS PRESS    SAN FRANCISCO

Cover design by John Herreid

© 2020 by Ignatius Press, San Francisco
All rights reserved
ISBN 978-1-62164-306-7 (PB)
ISBN 978-1-64229-129-2 (eBook)
Library of Congress Control Number 2020935528
Printed in the United States of America ∞

# Contents

# Preface

The initial plan for this book was simple enough, though not perhaps straightforward. I was going to put together some dozens of essays I had written for the website Mere Comments, which is sponsored by the journal *Touchstone*, for which I have written essays since 2003. I would flesh out the essays and provide connective tissue, and so the thing would be born.

Some of the material here does come from my old writing, then, but most does not. That is because, the more I wrote, the more urgently did I feel the need to address the unreality of our time, which seems like a bottomless crater. Every time we reach a new low, and we think to catch our breath and try to find a way up the crater walls, the floor collapses again beneath us, and we are lower than ever before. Many have said to me, "Surely modern man must now see that he cannot logically hold these positions at once." You cannot, logically, say that there are no differences between a man and a woman, and that somebody can be a woman trapped in a man's body. But who ever said that a commitment to unreality was going to be logical? In fact, the more that a commitment flies in the face of what is obviously real, the more perplexed the knots you must tie yourself up in to hold it, the more fiercely will your commitment be, and when the crater caves in again, you will be glad, glad indeed, because each new offense to reason and reality will startle the world, and you will enjoy that small interval of apparent rest. Because the world can hardly address the new unreality when it has not yet recovered from the old one.

George Orwell once wrote that if you hear everyone in the newspapers saying something, you can be reasonably sure it is false. Orwell did not have the advantage of the internet, which spreads lies at the speed of light, and multiplies them by millions a day. I take for granted that if everybody is saying something, and if that something is not part of the universal heritage of man, it is almost certainly false; and it is usually a falsehood too, a conscious lie, or a lie that has so deeply embedded itself into the mass mind that we accept it as we breathe in bad air.

My sense of the task at hand, then, sharpened as I wrote. We dwell in Unreal City. We all dwell there. We have all been dulled and deadened by the unreal. But if God is real, then to turn away from God is to leap into unreality, and that is pretty much the definition of evil. To believe in God, but to pretend for the sake of political action or moneymaking or schooling or marriage that he is not real, is to tell yourself a convenient lie, and to compromise the integrity of whatever good you are setting out to do. For we must always return to the questions of fact. If God exists, then the city that does not know God can hardly be expected to know itself. If good and evil exist, then all the bigots in the world will not change the fact, whether the bigots hold to what is good for the wrong reasons, or for understandable reasons hold to what is evil. The prussic acid is deadly and does not care for your opinion. If man and woman are what they are, attempts to fashion a society that denies that reality will be like trying to build a skyscraper out of cotton candy. It will hardly have enough of an essence even to collapse.

The problem is not that people are dull. Clever people

who begin from false premises will produce monsters. The problem is not even that our hold upon reality is slender. It has never been firm. It is that now, in our supposedly enlightened time, we have declared that an insistence upon reality is to be condemned. We do not therefore believe things that are false. We believe in *falsehood*. We do not merely believe in gods that do not exist. We believe in *un-being*. Some people call themselves Christians but believe in believing, as if God were a hobby, or a convenience, like a public restroom. Some people, atheists, believe in unbelieving, as if they could evade the questions of God's existence, and of the reality of good and evil, and of the nature and the destiny of man, by smirking and scoffing like ill-bred adolescents. I aim to call them out.

I believe in the Father, the Son, and the Holy Spirit. They are the rock of Truth. That is a claim as to fact. Cities can be built upon rock. Nothing can be built upon the lies we tell ourselves now. But we hunker down in Unreal City, and this book is a critique of its walls that do not stand, its towers that lean and creak, its doors that neither open nor close, its citizens that are not citizens, and its essence, which is the thing that is not.

# Unreality 101

I am looking at a book. It is hefty, clothbound, more than a thousand large two-columned pages, with print that is small and smaller, and plenty of black-and-white pictures. Inside it I find various forms of man's encounter with reality, including the reality of his own being, and of God.

In the book there is a matter-of-fact, cut-by-cut, fall-by-fall account of an attempt by three men to scale Mount Saint Elias, the second-tallest mountain in North America, and perhaps the most dangerous to climb, because its nearness to the ocean makes it subject to swings of bad weather, to snowstorms and the more dangerous melting of snow, with avalanches, and crevasses of hundreds or thousands of feet lurking beneath what looks like a flat white plain. The climbers did not make it to the summit. Six men from the party of explorers did not even make it to shore but were drowned when their boats capsized in a storm off Yakutat Bay.

There is a long appreciation of the poetry of the nineteenth century, not only in English but in French, German, and Italian, full of subtle analysis of the "subjective" spirit of Romanticism, what it offers and what it threatens to overpower or distort. Readers are expected to know who Byron was and what his poetry was about, and Shelley, Keats, Wordsworth, Tennyson, Arnold, Mrs. Browning, Lamartine, Daudet, Hugo, Heine, Leopardi, Goethe, and many more.

There are short stories, and new entries in serialized novels, eagerly awaited by people who had been following along for months. There are essays on the Civil War, most written by the combatants themselves. There are essays on the art of the Renaissance masters Carpaccio and Luini, the organization of German cities, the Chicago World's Fair in 1893, and far more, far more. No book like it is published now. I suppose that many college professors would find it daunting to read, and for most college students it would be incomprehensible, just because of the great funds of general knowledge its many and various authors expected literate people to possess. But it was not written for the college educated. I would wager that half of its authors themselves were not college educated. It is a bound volume of six months of the *Century Magazine*, from June through November 1892.

The most fundamental thing that separates its readers from us is that even a rich man in 1892 had daily encounters with the sweet and stubborn rocks and trees of reality. If you were in New York and you wanted to get to Boston, you rode a horse or you took a train, and either way, you had reality, big and strong and sometimes dangerous, to reckon with. The horses needed constant care. They needed to be fed, watered, and curried. The horse had no "check stomach" light. No alarm alerted you to the crack in the wooden carriage wheel that would give way when you hit the next sharp stone. The train was furious, and furiously hungry for fuel. Men, perfectly black with the smoke and dust, made a living shoveling coal into its belly. At every rail station you saw men, and so too on the rails themselves. The bell that let you know it was time to depart reminded you of the sledgehammers that drove in every spike for every tie, for thousands of miles all across the nation.

You find that muscular excitement in the *Century*, along

with plenty of warning voices, because the people were honest enough to see the dirt and the moral degradation that sometimes came in the wake of technological development. The most "progressive" among them were the most suspicious of any notion that better tools make better men, or that the governmental machine must inevitably grow more efficient and humane, just because we have better ways of storing ice than we used to have.

## Belial's Books

I cannot buy the *Century* at a bookstore. The *Century* printed essays by agnostics, sure; and you cannot publish the novels of Mark Twain and Henry James without brushing against their modern doubts. But the *Century* looked more than kindly upon the Christian faith. Its editors took for granted that the civilization itself depended upon the health of that faith. That too was reality speaking. There is no culture without a felt encounter with the divine. It is a contradiction in terms. There are mass habits, but no culture, because people lose the sense that they have anything of surpassing value to pass along.

What has happened in the meantime? Agnostic progressives from the early twentieth century believed that the Christian faith would recede as engagement with reality came more urgently to the fore. The truth has been the reverse. Faith has not been a compromise with reason, as they had thought, or a tramp hitching a ride on reason's train. Faith has been the leader of reason, its promoter and protector. I see as much when I notice what people now read, if they read at all.

I do not care anymore to go to bookstores, such as still

exist, that sell new books. I recall some years ago when I poked my nose into a store run by one of the nation's two great booksellers, Belial's or something of that sort. It has, I believe, gone out of business, and its main rival is none too healthy, either. As I rummaged through the aisles, I found myself growing testy and irritated, and that made me wonder: Why, when I used to love drowning an hour or two in a bookstore, did I hate going there now? What was it about Belial's (and his rival Beelzebub's) that made the flesh creep? Why did I feel that I had entered a madhouse?

It might have been that form of unreality that we call porn. Belial—I mean the original, *Diabolus cornutus*—about forty years ago started putting up ugly windowless "adult" bookshops for nasty little children when their bodies but not their souls outgrew the woodshed. But that sort of thing never corrupted more than a small portion of the populace, and those were probably dragging Belial's fetters along already. So there was not, for Belial, a lot of profit to show.

Still, the dirty bookstores set a standard of excellence. If, for instance, something fell short of the absolute human degradation found in the "adult" store, it could be sold elsewhere, with the justification, "At least it isn't as bad as . . .", and you might complete the sentence as you liked. An interesting sales maneuver, one that turned a steamy second-rate pornograph by an impotent man named Lawrence into the equivalent of a Victorian lady going hatless. For as people grew more and more accustomed to "not as bad as", those few souls who were honest about their debauchery had to sink further and further down the abyss, if only to separate themselves from the pretenders. All this was fine with Belial, as it allowed him to remove inventory from Skin City to shopping malls, to the grocery store (a great boon to the gentle sex, many of whom might shy away from an "adult" store, but who pick up a *Cosmopolitan* on the way out with a can of pork and beans and a packet of powdered brimstone), and now, at last, to the staid old bookstore. In the land of Belial, even the old church ladies leer. I have heard that a group of "mums" in England have produced their own porn flicks for their sons to watch, as being "not as bad as" the really crude things on sale elsewhere. They would be ideal customers at Belial's Books.

Belial does not care whom he makes his money from, so sure enough there was a section devoted to Christianity, with Bibles of all flavors, for every need. The word of God comes tricked out in style, in our land of the commercial. These Bibles sat alongside something called Christian Literature, by which apparently are signified glossy-covered novels about strange creatures straining to be hobbits. Belial will gladly demote the faith to a selection for them as likes that sort of thing. Belial does not sell a lot of sermons, though. You were not going to find Donne on Emergent Occasions, or C. H. Spurgeon, or Jeremy Taylor, or Lancelot Andrewes. You would find a lot of Christian Self-Help, which is awfully convenient, since it would allow you to slide easily into the interminable Self section, covering Self in Lotus Position, Self with Herbs, Self in the Zodiac, Self as God, and Self with Self (the latter going by name of "Gay and Lesbian", prominently labeled for the benefit of children). Erotics was nearby, with an aisle of its own. I am not sure whether the Song of Songs was shelved there.

Belial's Books was as noisy as its provenance. I mean the visual noise: the garish jackets, the flesh, the gaudy expensive hardcover books on everything from Botticelli to baseball, some of them very good books, but many of them clearly put out by a book factory somewhere below, full of bright pictures and few words and less sense. Indeed, taking a cue from those places called "libraries", from whose rejects I have derived my collection of issues of the *Century*, Belial devoted half his store to anything but books. So you could buy recordings of Bach or Mozart, or gangsta rap; or toys for tots; or *Playboy* calendars, or pictures of the Madonna and Child. Why should Belial discriminate? *That* is his genius. Everything may go for a price, as Judas once understood. There is no inherent value in anything.

For example, in the least sulfurous section of the store, the corner devoted to History, you could find some interesting work, mingled among Herodotus and Thucydides and the classics. You would also find silly snarling twaddle, from both political corners (and, I suppose, from the center, except that twaddle from the center makes up for its silliness by being both cowardly and dull, so that Belial himself, with Satan as his hawker, could never sell a lot of it). You would find a hateful pack of lies against Pius XII, right next to a good but wholly unnecessary book written to address the pack of lies. Such a waste of talent and effort. It was downhill from History. I will not start on the Literature section, except to note that Belial did allow a certain translation of the *Inferno* to grace his shelves, confident that no one would take it seriously. After all, people who have lived through the hundred years that gave us Auschwitz and the Cultural Revolution and many millions of unborn children crushed or dismembered every year cannot possibly believe, with Jefferson of all people, that God is just.

I shop for my books in antique stores now. You may recognize the sort of books I buy: dull old things with plain pasteboard covers and few or no pictures. I found one that same day. It was a charming little book of about three hundred pages, containing the letters of Teddy Roosevelt to his family. "Blessed Kermit," begins one, addressing the lad at boarding school in Groton, and "Darling Kermit," begins another, describing how the kitten Tom Quartz mistook for a dog the trousers of Speaker of the House Joe Cannon. The scratches were real, as was the wary respect that these rival members of the same party had for one another.

I recall a fine book from another moral universe, called *Real Boys*, by one Henry Shute, who was one of those real boys and who really led the boyish life he describes, in the prep school town of Exeter, New Hampshire. He was not one of the elites in that boarding school. Exeter was his own town. But he had something of the same real education that the rich boys had, and that comes across at the end of his saga of boyish adventures—swimming, skating, snowball fights, flirting with girls, gathering hazelnuts in the woods, playing baseball and dozens of games whose names we no longer recognize, and a thousand more things from dawn to dusk. You can infer something about that real education from the way he ends the book. He pretends that he, nicknamed "Plupy" in those days in which every boy had a nickname, was an ancient historian such as those boys would have read in their public school:

> In the ancient forays of the Gauls, it was the custom to look to all the able-bodied men for actual warfare, and leave the old and sick and worn-out men to tend the camp. It happened that there was always some man not old enough to shirk duty, but of no value in the rude sports, the forced marches, and the fierce conflicts of the time.
>
> Such a one was usually employed to chronicle the events, to sing of the descriptions of battles and the prowess of heroes. This position was usually accorded him not because he was in any degree better fitted for it, but because

he was fit for nothing else. And so, perhaps for similar reasons, this has fallen to Plupy's lot, and if his description pleases, he is indeed fortunate and grateful.[1]

That was a hundred years ago. My grandparents were already grown up when it was written. For its eloquence, its humility, its good humor, its childlike delight in real things and real people, it might have been a hundred centuries ago —so far does it seem from our time.

## Enrolling in Unreal

Where can we find reality on record? Where can we go following to its source some happy brook of what is real?

You might expect that investigation into the real would be the aim of a university education, even if you cannot reliably find it at a bookstore. It is not so.

As education has grown more political in its aim, so has it grown less truly educational, and more plainly unreal. Political persuasion has always partaken of the unreal. The Athenian tyrant Pisistratus once tried to win an election by dressing up a very tall woman, a stranger to Athens, as the goddess Athena and parading her in a carriage through the city, calling on all her devotees to vote for Pisistratus. I am glad to say that it did not work, so Pisistratus, an able statesman, had to seize power by irregular means. Hence he was a "tyrant", though that did not mean he was not a nice person. He was, as it turns out, a capable and farsighted ruler. Julius Caesar won the affection of his soldiers by his eminently successful and brutal campaigns in Gaul, which campaigns he made sure everyone would learn about, as he recorded them

[1] Henry A. Shute, *Real Boys* (New York: J.J. Little, 1905), p. 257.

himself. Nothing but the truth. Machiavelli, in *The Prince*, advised Lorenzo de' Medici that a prince should seize the great advantage of *appearing* to be virtuous, while all along he might be as faithless and ruthless as would serve his purposes. "Off goes his bonnet to an oyster-wench", grouses Shakespeare's Richard II, complaining about how the false and ambitious Henry Bolingbroke plays the crowds.[2]

As advertisers make their money persuading people that they want what they do not want, and need what they do not need, so the politician, especially in our time of constant noise, gains his power by keeping people in a continual state of fear, hatred, resentment, or vindictiveness, those passions so requisite for the common good. It is unreality. An education that is politicized makes young people less educable, insofar as they are caught up in the craze of the time. They will think that the world is going to hell. Of course it is going to hell. It has always been going to hell. A great part of the world has already staked its claims and laid its foundations in the ice.

We cannot get enough of unreality. It is like cotton candy to a greedy child, with mouth perfectly pink. A legislator from Oregon has recently proposed lowering the voting age to sixteen—years, not months, though many a young person in our time still sucks on the rubber nipple. Sixteen-year-old children should be permitted to vote, she says, "to protect their interests". They have no interests. They run no businesses, they have no investments, they are not married, they own no homes; their interests are merely what their teachers from mass entertainment, mass politics, and mass education

---

[2] *Richard II*, ed. Frances E. Dolan (New York: Penguin, 2007), act 1, scene 4, line 31.

say they are. The scandal here is not that the legislator is in error. People do make mistakes. It is that she has taken leave of her senses, and nobody has demanded her recall. It is as if she had proposed to build a three-story house out of noodles and thus instigated an argument about whether the noodles should be linguine or lasagna. Unreality already is the political air we breathe. The problem is not whether we can get such children to think responsibly about reality. Aside from the exceptional, they never will. They cannot. They have insufficient experience. Our problem is whether we can get sixty-year-old children to cease brooding upon unreality.

Not likely. The current Speaker of the House, Nancy Pelosi, has given the Oregonian proposal her approval, and there are moves in a couple of other states also to lower the voting age. They are being spearheaded by women. Now, I would like to take note of a fact. Women are not naturally sour and skeptical, and therefore they are not naturally given to strip their motives of their accoutrements and décor. "Mirror, mirror on the wall, who is the fairest of them all?" asks the queen, who is sure of the answer already. Such queens can be bought wholesale in a time when no one dare say anything critical about the sex without incurring the charge of misogyny. But women are given to *enthusiasm*. Think of Carry A. Nation. Think of Salem. More about such enthusiasm later.

When my daughter was young, she would often be asked, not usually by fellow homeschoolers, why she kept reading *The Lord of the Rings*. I told her to reply, "Because I want to know what's going on in the world." Tolkien's fantasy was rooted in truth. He had studied millennia of human wisdom. He had experienced in his own person the misery of the first world war, and through the person of his son

Christopher the misery of the second. He was an English don with ink on his hands and dirt under his fingernails—a solid man, not to be tossed hither and yon by political enthusiasm. I wanted that same solidity for my daughter, and my wife and I knew that it would not come from school.

For you do not go to school to learn about what is real. In this regard I recall a discussion I once had with a Catholic men's group at the college where I taught. One of the young fellows told me that his professor in Introduction to Sociology, a typical course assigned during orientation to unsuspecting freshmen, expressed her disdain for what was at that time the school's twenty-credit Development of Western Civilization Program, required of all students. In that course they would read Homer, Plato, Aristotle, Cicero, Virgil, Saint Paul, Saint Augustine—and much more, just in the first of the four semesters. "You should be studying something that will be of use to you in the Real World," she said, "like feminist sociology." One of the telltales of unreality is surely a failure to see how silly you are. Homer, Plato, Aristotle, Cicero, Virgil, Saint Paul, Saint Augustine —no use for the life of the mind, apparently. And everyone is silly; there are the fools who know it, and the more ridiculous fools who do not. Colleges are largely staffed by the latter.

*Homo academicus saecularis sinister*, the creature beside whom I have spent all my adult life, is a source of endless entertainment, like a child with wobbly consonants trying to speak like Gladstone. I could not repress my merriment. "If somebody said that to me", I laughed, "who was a construction worker, or who went down in the mines, or quarried rock, or built roads, I would say, 'Fellow, you are wrong about that', but at least I'd say there was something to what he had said." But *Homo academicus saecularis sinister* does not have much regard for builders and miners. *HASS* never drives down the highway saying, "How fortunate I am! I don't have to break my back in the sun, and I get three months of the year off, and I am paid quite well compared with what a man or a woman who does something absolutely necessary is paid, as for instance the men who rolled the asphalt on this road I am speeding on." Indeed, *HASS* will complain about never being paid in accordance with his intelligence, which, according to the most reliable testimony, that of *HASS*—who should know best, after all—is astonishingly high.

When I hear a phrase like "the Real World", used in that polemical sense, I confess that I fall into the sin of detraction. I detract fifteen points of intelligence and ten points of common sense from my interlocutor. Should it be followed by such phrases as "today's society" or "the global marketplace" or "thinking outside the box", I inevitably turn to an object of greater interest: a child playing in a sandbox, a retriever wagging his doggy tail, or the purple streaks of stratus cloud gathering in the west. I dearly hope that my students will never consider the sand-furrowing child, or the galumphing retriever, or the setting sun to be anything other than deeply Real, mysteriously and beautifully and achingly Real, and I hope too that their encounter with the great poetry and art of the West, not to mention that perennial philosophy of Aristotle, and that wisdom-seeking eros of Plato, and the word of God itself, will confirm them in their love for that Reality.

One of the students observed that the professor was overeducated. Alas, that is not true. Where were the overeducated men and women who wrote for my issues of the *Century*? Was one of them George Kennan Sr., reporting firsthand about the prison camps in Siberia under Czar Alexander? Was one of them Nikola Tesla, the scientist, attempting to introduce to English readers the poetry of his Serbian countryman Zmai Iovan Iovanovich? Was one of them Mariana Griswold Van Rensselaer, writing sensitively about native forms of sacred architecture in New England churches? Those people were schooled in reality and in man's encounter with it. Not one of them was a college professor when they wrote those articles. Yet they could hardly be professors now, at our colleges, such as they are.

If I were to take a truck driver who knew nothing of the Renaissance to the Sistine Chapel, he would not be so foolish, I am sure, as to say that it was all just a swarm of naked people falling over themselves. He would feel his ignorance intensely. He would sense that there was a mystery there to which he had hope someone might introduce him, to lead him by the hand, saying, "Notice the electric space between the finger of God and the finger of Adam", or "See how Michelangelo has painted his own face in the sagging skin held up by Saint Bartholomew." My friend might be slightly undereducated to appreciate an hour in the Sistine Chapel, and who among us, for that hour, would not be? But the college professor who sniffs at the *Epic of Gilgamesh*, Hesiod, Homer, Aeschylus, Sophocles, Pindar, Plato, Aristotle, Livy, Cicero, Virgil, Marcus Aurelius, Augustine, the Torah, the Psalms, the Gospels, and the letters of Saint Paul, in a course since mauled by the campus politicians, is *not* overeducated. That professor is *undereducated,* and *overschooled,* a deadening duo. Deadening, but common enough from what I see, and especially common among people who reduce all matters to contemporary partisan politics, as *HASS* is wont to do.

I no longer teach at that school, which in recent years has slipped considerably into sexual unreality, but at a small and doggedly faithful and *real* Catholic school in New Hampshire, Magdalen College of the Liberal Arts. My sophomores will in a few days be going to Rome, where they will spend several months studying literature and art, and never will they be so smugly and absurdly serious as to suppose that Michelangelo and Augustine have nothing to teach them about what is real.

## *To Market, To Market!*

Yet I know I am trying to breast the tide. It has been going on for a long time, this collapse of college education into unreality.

When I was a freshman at Princeton in 1977, we had a full week by way of introduction to college life. Most of it was pleasant. I recall with much fondness an old storytelling curator of Princetoniana, the Reverend Frederick Fox. A dozen other boys and I duly stole the clapper from the cupola of Nassau Hall, as all freshmen were supposed to try to do. We had athletic competitions against the sophomores, called "Cane Spree". We were all brought into a single large hall to be addressed by a senior on the school's Honor Code. The various departments scheduled their own introductions for interested students. I attended the one given by the Mathematics Department and heard a fascinating lecture on the calculus of variations, called "How to Catch Fish with a Boat".

We were divided also into small groups, one day, for an hour, to talk about sex. I do not remember any rules. It was a discussion, and it was deeply disappointing. The consensus was that there was no such thing as sexual morality, except that something called "love" ought to be involved. That, however, was too much for one burly and bearded fellow, who declared that he saw nothing wrong with "cold and mechanical" sex, so long as both people agreed to it. So ended that venture into moral philosophy. Princeton was, morally, a dark place growing darker, but I do not believe that it was yet an *unreal place*, for the life of the mind. Truth was not only a defense. It was the thing to be sought.

I advance the reel nearly thirty years. It is 2007. My daughter is attending orientation at Providence College. It is a two-day affair designed to introduce students to the life of the mind, not by reminding them of the precious heritage of scholarship to which their professors will have devoted their energies and what portion of talent nature has seen fit to bestow upon them, but by advising them on What to Do If Your Roommate Is Drunk and Unconscious, How Not to Overload the Washing Machines, and, alas, What Constitutes Rape. I have only the sketchiest details about that last part of the initiation. My daughter chose that moment to appear to have to use the bathroom, which is one of the unquestioned privileges of a young lady.

None of this was free, in either important sense of the word: she had to attend, under threat of losing her spot in the freshman class, and her father had to cough up a couple hundred dollars for the privilege. The orientation program was cheerful and chirpy enough, and she did meet a few people whom it was unlikely she would run into again. She also had the pleasure of sitting next to a friendly young Nepalese man who could not help scowling when a patronizing video informed him that "diversity" was important at Providence College, that some people were white and some people were black, some people were Catholic and some were Protestant and some were Jews, and some—and a special point was made of this—some people were gay. Ah, the joy of being a mascot!

It could have been far worse, I know. Providence College did at that time try to be a Catholic school; that is, it tried to be Catholic, and it tried to be a school. The organizers of the orientation, most of them friendly women in the dutifully anagrammatic Students Active in Leadership (SAIL) office, did not really mean to undermine either the life of the mind or the Catholic faith, about which subjects they may as well have been as innocent as golden retrievers, nor did they mean to reject the solemn inculcation of such natural virtues as temperance, courage, and chastity, whereof no doubt they would have approved, if some kind soul would have but once made their acquaintance with the notions. But such people do not simply *work* at the college—and now I am speaking of every college in the land. They peg the college into its proper hole. They and their helpers in Residence Life and Student Affairs and this Center and that Epicycle do more to define what it means to go to school than any professor does, and perhaps, though this is still debatable, more than do all the professors put together. And the professors hardly deserve any better. They too work on the mental demolition team.

Of course it is all unreality. How long it will survive as such, I do not know. For the schools have set themselves up in an enviable position. They are what are called "rent seekers". I like to illustrate it by a passage in Edmund Spenser's *The Faerie Queene*. I beg the reader's pardon, as the language is slightly difficult; Nathaniel Hawthorne used to read *The Faerie Queene* aloud to his wife and children of an evening, but that was in a time of undoubted intellectual eclipse. The scene is a bridge, controlled by a wicked Saracen named Pollente. The name is a bilingual pun: from Latin *pollens*, "powerful", and from English *poll*, "head". For a "poll tax" is a tax not on your income or property but upon your poll—your bean, your noggin—and to poll people is to count heads.

The Saracen takes advantage of his position to squeeze both
rich and poor:

> And daily he his wrongs increaseth more,
> For never wight he lets to pass that way,
> Over his bridge, albe he rich or poor,
> But he him makes his passage-penny pay:
> Else he doth hold him back or beat away.
> Thereto he hath a groom of evil guise
> Whose scalp is bare, that bondage doth bewray,
> Which pills and polls the poor in piteous wise;
> But he himself upon the rich doth tyrannize.[3]

Spenser has put his finger on the evils of an economic bot-
tleneck. We might call it a monopoly, a cartel, or a turnpike.
The principle is the same. You control the only means by
which ordinary people can get something ordinary done.
They must cross the river at this point, and you hold the
bridge. They need coal for their foundries, and you own all
the mines. Their children need to pass through your credentialing agency if they wish to become professionals of
any sort, and you combine, in an effective cartel, with other
schools and with the government (which pours out upon
you money it has confiscated from both rich and poor), to
keep costs as high as possible; and professional groups, in
part to keep government overseers at bay, permit you to do
their credentialing and testing for them. There is no other
way for someone to become a doctor, a lawyer, a banker, or
even an insurance salesman such as my high-school-educated
father was, without putting his house in hock over the gables
to pay you off. If ever a Marxist analysis were needed, it is

---

[3] Edmund Spenser, *The Faerie Queen*, bk. 5, canto 2, st. 6.

here, to show up the Marxists themselves. But it is easy to be liberal with other people's money, especially when you seize so much of it yourself.

It will come crashing down when some enterprising person finds the ford upstream. That is my hope. Reality will triumph.

But much will have been lost before then. My mind turns to a room in an old library in the small town of Eastport, Maine, once a thriving port, the easternmost town in the United States. I see what used to be the main room, built in that old style for libraries, the marble pilasters faintly reminiscent of Greece and Rome. In one corner there is a large hutch, a built-in bookshelf behind glass doors; forbidding tomes of nineteenth-century Maine history rest there, resolving into the dust. In another corner, hung high upon the wall, stands a lovely painting in the Hudson Valley style. Its title reads *Cherry Valley, Pennsylvania*, and the hand-carved and gilt frame alone is probably worth thousands. But the rest of the room is noisy with triviality: plasticine shelves for periodicals, all blaring color and vulgarity, the new pictograms for a people too impatient to read and too intemperate to think.

When I asked the librarian about the painting, she said she did not know who the painter was, nor was she interested. Eventually it will go. If the library staff are smart, they will sell it at auction, to buy a scanner or something else of eternal use. The books too will go. If the staff are smart, they will send them to a mausoleum in Augusta: a Maine Historical Mausoleum, next to an Art Mausoleum; those places where truly popular culture goes after it is dead. The transfer will open up that corner for the ghastly thing called Young Adult Fiction, no question.

Do not, I say, expect professors to lead the battle to preserve a real culture. I once found myself listening in perplexity as a young professor regaled her colleagues on the merits of the "e-portfolio", an electronic scrapbook for undergraduates who wish to track their heroic conquest of such things as "intercultural values" and "leadership" and "skills" and "active learning". Into this portfolio, this scrapbook, this collage that is to be the acme of four years and two hundred thousand dollars' worth of pretended instruction, students deposit their papers, or, more commonly, their PowerPoint presentations, or photos from two weeks of erudition in Namibia, or slick images culled from the internet and pasted in with appropriate captions. They are to comment upon their progress, hugging themselves for growing in wisdom and understanding, or at least for scrambling up a few tricks that will make them marketable. It is not the discovery of the self. It is the advertisement of a "self", a set of poses.

No doubt, some students might profit from saving their papers and glancing at the old ones once in a while, to see how far they have risen, or slid, as the case may be (and it was remarkable that the gracious presenter never considered the possibility that a student might, by dint of his own hard work and the persevering care of his professors, progressively lose the modest stock of reason he had entered school withal). And I can see the purpose in opening such portfolios—at best, forgivably youthful forays into a field of knowledge vastly more intricate and more demanding than the student can imagine—to the comments of a trusted professor. But there was something missing from this student-centered—which is to say, self-centered—game of Accomplishing Great Things.

Education was missing. When comes that moment when the student confronts the stark grandeur of intellectual reality and says, "Everything I thought I knew was wrong or incomplete. All my work has been trash"? Or how can a student track his "progress" in wisdom, when that is the very last thing that a wise man will do; whereas fools will spend all day cataloguing their conquests? Where is the sense of something unspeakably beautiful, or unfathomable, or holy; some object of study that makes all talk of "progress" sound absurd? I know a lot more about literature now than I did when I was in college, and the main thing I know is that what I do not know still far outweighs what I do. My omissions have names like Proust and Borges. Would that make a good PowerPoint slide for a vamping come-on, to beguile some John the Employer?

In my universe, after the professor who taught me Dante (and who has forgotten more about that irascible Florentine than I have ever known) looks back upon his distinguished career—I am speaking about Robert Hollander, the greatest student of Dante in the United States—he says, "I think I am finally beginning to understand the *Divine Comedy*." No smugness there, no presumption; and isn't it always the very finest of teachers, those who know the most, who have so keen an awareness of the dread beauty of their subject that they never do presume to have mastered it? Life is short, said Hippocrates, but the art is long. Vision is narrow, and reality vast.

That is the universe of the few teachers who ever made any difference in my life. In our time it is smothered under the unreal. By the many millions, it is smothered under slogans, folders, cheap Parisian *bons mots* like "deconstructive" and "transgressive", mixed up with the clunky noun boxcars of educanto, logjams like "student learning goals" and "learning progress assessment", trains with all the elegance of German abstraction and none of the efficiency; too much Chanel on a tart from Dortmund. That, with courses in such things as "Shakespeare *and* . . .", meaning "Not Shakespeare but Gender", or "Not Shakespeare but Race", will suffice for one to secure a well-remunerated position somewhere. We used to have steamy plush hotels for this sort of thing—they were a lot less trouble, and they did much less damage to the common good.

## Them Bad Old Puritans

I am sometimes asked whether well-intended secularists can assist us in returning schools and colleges to reality. I do not think so.

As I have suggested, agnostics in the nineteenth century believed they could give up faith in God and yet maintain a firm commitment to the truth. That has not proved to be the case. Jesus said, "I am the way, the truth, and the life", and indeed Gregory the Great's favorite name for Jesus is simply *Truth*. We can imagine being *true* to a Person, who looks out upon us with his all-seeing eyes. It is almost impossible to imagine being true to an abstraction. We can conceive of it, but all images recede, and so does the passion for faithfulness. I want very dearly to be true to Christ, and that passion can serve to check me at every pass, at every opportunity for trimming, ducking, sliding, and speaking double. What is the alternative? "To *thine own self* be true", said Polonius, who was a canting, wheedling, tedious, eavesdropping, silly old man.[4]

The hardest of hard scientists may remain true to the laws of their discipline, but only because brute reality would condemn them for their errors or their lies, and with devastating

[4] William Shakespeare, *Hamlet*, ed. T. J. B. Spencer (New York: Penguin Books, 1996), act 1, scene 3, line 78.

speed. The airplane does not fly. But the further they are from such checks, the more likely they are to engage happily in unreality, and that is especially true when their disciplines have admitted into their midst the political huckster, standing on his soapbox, swaying his (or her) capacious belly left and right, gesticulating about the end of the world, or the beginning of a new and improved world, or both at once. We have seen such huckstering in mathematical models for climate science, and in interpreting the data. Since none of us has a time machine, we cannot check the claims against results to be seen long in the future, and that gives the scientific politician, on whichever side he happens to fall, all the room he needs to ply his deceptive trade. Nor does it help matters if he himself is the first person he deceives.

And scientists are men, such as we. They too empty their wallets for Bacon's idols of the marketplace. They do not, in the first instance, go where reality leads. They go where the herd leads. It should abash them and everyone else to read about how stubbornly resisted were Pasteur's claims that disease was carried by living things, which we call, by way of a wholly misleading analogy, "germs", that is, seeds. For the materialist position of the time held to the old notion of abiogenesis: you could get maggots from a rotting corpse, and insect grubs from the sun-warmed mud of the Nile, and so too you could get terrible diseases from bad air and the disharmony of your inner organs and your blood. It is dreadful to think of how many thousands of women died postpartum in those charnel houses called hospitals because doctors and nurses held to the old ideology and would not disinfect their hands.

And when you move away from those few fields, compromised as they often are by human error and perversity, all bets are off the table. The new director of the

National Gallery of Art, in Washington, D.C., has recently
announced that her aim for the museum, which is one of
the finest in the world, will not primarily be to show great
art but to promote a political agenda. The reader can easily predict the terms: "gender equality", "diversity", "social
justice". In other words, having long abandoned her commitment to truth, she has no more commitment to beauty,
or to art for its own sake; she has become a political huckster, a propagandist, and the nation's taxpayers will finance
the propaganda. But that is what you get across all the humanities and social sciences. As soon as someone says that
truth is socially constructed, unless he is simply addled, he
has already declared himself to be a liar, or at least to be in
no great opposition to liars.

Which brings me to a lecture I once heard on the Puritans.
It was given by a candidate for a job teaching contemporary
fiction. The young man was lively enough, and willing to
entertain criticism; and he seemed also to enjoy the peculiar-
ities of the literary craft, which was a great mark in his favor:
it is by no means certain, and sometimes not even probable,
that a teacher of literature will *like literature* for itself. He was
discussing how the novelist Thomas Pynchon, in *Gravity's
Rainbow*, was revisiting the views of his Puritan ancestors,
particularly those of one William Pynchon, who rebelled
modestly against the rigorous Calvinism of the governor of
Connecticut, Thomas Hooker.

The candidate did a good job describing that Calvinism,
and the strange psychological double bind that it encour-
ages. For one is to be simultaneously assured of one's salvation, yet one must never presume that that salvation is certain. Without the comforting and tangible communicators
of grace called sacraments, Calvinism can—I am not saying
that it necessarily or even usually does—turn obsessively

introspective, as one reassesses, again and again, the status
of that blessed assurance. To give them credit, the Puritans and their sympathizers were aware of the pitfall. They
wrote about it frequently enough. See for instance Red Cross
Knight's encounter with the wily anti-theologian Despair in
*The Faerie Queene*.

Yet our candidate seemed to believe that it would have
been easy for the old Puritans to move, as he put it, "a little
bit to the left" (notice the political terminology) and admit
that the grace of God might come to those who were outside their covenanted community, and even to those who
otherwise seemed to belong squarely among the reprobates.
In saying so, he made no attempt to justify the movement
in terms that the Puritans would have acknowledged. His
concern was not *the truth*. It seemed not to enter his mind
that perhaps the Puritans might have been *correct* about grace
and salvation. It is rather like what people wish the Catholic
Church would do as regards their preferred mode of sexual
release, hitherto recognized as immoral. There is a strange
unreality about the wish. No one would say that we could
alter the nature of a melanoma by calling it a beauty mark.

So then, the Puritans, and America, could have taken another path, William Pynchon's path. They could have es-
chewed the "rigorist" position, the "conservative" position.
They could have, the candidate said, admitted that "alterity"
could be a gift; that sometimes what looks like spiritual sloth
might instead be a wise suspension of "strict orthodoxy" in
the face of other ways of life.

That sounds nice. When the evangelist David Livingstone
made his lonesome and dangerous way into the heart of the
Congo, he witnessed human slavery, torture, and the glee of
cannibalism. I have read a first-person account of the intoxi-
cating delight of a Congolese tribe that severed the heads of

the slaves they had captured, after a sufficient period of tor-
ment, obscenities, and public humiliation. They would toss
the heads in the air as a prize, and then they would get down
to the serious bloody business of the feast. The Englishman
who saw it, one Thomas Villiers, following in the steps of
Livingstone and Henry Morton Stanley, determined that he
would do all in his power to see to it that no similar gala
would ever transpire in any region under his authority—
his quite tenuous authority. Unfortunately, Villiers had not
been trained to appreciate the gifts of alterity, and the wise
suspension of "strict orthodoxy" in the matter of the festive
and culinary.

I wanted to say to the candidate who pumped for alterity,
"As, for instance, academics might welcome conservatives
into their midst", but I refrained. Instead I asked whether
America had not indeed taken that very path that the candidate said we had rejected. For better or for worse, doctrinal
differences among the denominations were already blurry by
the time Jonathan Edwards came along (1703–1758), and
then the Wesleyan revival (ca. 1741), too, ensured that Puritanism would never be the majority position again, not even
in New England. By the middle of the nineteenth century,
what used to be congregational Puritanism was careering
over into Unitarianism, where it seems to be now—there,
or in a kind of Arianism with chicken soup: a belief in Jesus
as a worthy teacher, and in social amelioration by means of
local charity and, more frequently, government machinery.

It is hard to imagine that there was a time when Ralph
Waldo Emerson and Henry Ward Beecher were leading
lights of American religion. They were serious souls who
wore their enlightened morality like royal robes, but their
religion very lightly. Revivals of American religious life
have been roused by a reaction against our constant national

tendency to gloss over differences in doctrine. That tendency
is a function of our go-getter's impatience with the careful
distinction that theology demands. The reason why there
are people called "fundamentalists" (a term that nowadays,
depending on the speaker, can denote, of all things, a Catholic who believes in the teachings of the Church) is precisely
because we Americans have always muddled our theology
and taken on every new idea or fad, sometimes with a shrug,
and sometimes with the excitement of a know-it-all sucker
who has bought up all the really effective elixir, yes indeed!

But what amused me most about the presentation was
the candidate's use of terms like "conservative" and "right-
wing" and, as a pejorative, "orthodox" (naturally, without
asking whether the position he was labeling orthodox was
in fact correct). The Puritans were conservative? Strange
way to look at them. Tell it to William Laud and Charles I,
both of whom met the headsman's ax, swung by the Puritan, not least for their affinity with ancient Romish forms of
worship. Tell it to the "old believers" who could no longer
stage their mystery plays, those rollicking affairs that Shakespeare himself saw when he was a boy. Tell it to Shakespeare's recusant father, and to his recusant daughter. Tell it
to Shakespeare.

And John Robinson's crew, those who commissioned and
stocked and boarded the Mayflower, conservative? They
who dabbled in setting up a Plato's Republic in Massachusetts
before they saw that it was an unworkable and unbiblical
fantasy (to paraphrase the wise words of their governor,
William Bradford)? It might take a long and thoughtful essay to describe in precisely which ways the Puritans might
justifiably be considered "conservative", but that essay was
not forthcoming. "Conservative" was simply a synonym for
"backward", "narrow-minded", "mean", "fearful of other-

ness", and so on, and then of course conservatives, whose souls are about as interesting as wooden stumps, would become responsible for slavery and the ravaging of the native peoples. Nothing subtle or complex can be stamped upon a button for a political convention. There is no room for it.

The Romans, who were as open to "otherness" as any people in the history of the world have ever been—far more open to it than hypocritical academics are—also *conquered* those others they were open to. The pacifist Amish, by contrast, want as little as possible to do with "others". The Puritans at Plymouth believed that the Indians were almost undoubtedly all going to hell; but they learned a couple of agricultural tricks from them, and they treated them remarkably well, punishing severely anybody who took advantage of them. Bradford was justly proud of his community's peaceful dealings with the local natives.

The Spanish, on the other hand, had immeasurably more to do with the Indians than the Puritans ever had. The Jesuit, Dominican, and Franciscan missionaries, unlike the Puritans, did not believe that the Indians in their fallen nature were entirely deprived of the light of God—so they were "open" to the possibility of salvation for these people. Yet Spaniards also established the plantation system, in which the Indians were exploited as serfs or outright slaves.

The candidate did understand that he was playing fast and loose with political jargon, applying it far out of context; he did say that Puritans were very far from the tight-lipped Victorian sorts that their descendant the novelist Hawthorne made them out to be, and he gave examples. Would that he could have extended the same courtesy to Calvinists, or to all those people, whomever he might have imagined them to be, whom he called conservative.

A commitment to truth, when it comes to the messiness

of human history, practically rules out political posturing. Or political posturing rules out a commitment to truth.

I saw another example of it the next day, when my wife and I watched a BBC production of Charles Dickens' *Hard Times* from 1994. It did the same foolish thing that the candidate did, with the same blithe unconcern for truth. Dickens has cast Thomas Gradgrind, the educational "reformer" of the book, as a confirmed materialist utilitarian. "Facts, facts, facts!" cries Mr. Gradgrind. "Teach these children nothing but facts!" Gradgrind is a caricature of the materialists Jeremy Bentham and the elder Mill. He is *not* Thomas Arnold or Matthew Arnold. He does not believe in the life of the imagination; he believes we will be saved by economy, not by treasuring the best of what has been thought, said, and done in the world. He would fit in well with our current despisers of the humanities and the liberal arts.

So, in the film, what party does Mr. Gradgrind run for, to represent his district in Parliament? Why, the Tory Party. It is not in the book, but who cares? The Utilitarians, and the despisers of the classical education of the old schools, and the laissez-faire economists were Whigs, not Tories. That is not to say that there were not plenty of humanitarian reformers among the Whigs, but it was the Tory prime minister Disraeli, not the Whig Gladstone, who wrote about the two Britains, rich and poor. Dickens wisely refrains from telling us which party Gradgrind represents, and he is right to refrain, because the great totalizing schemers of the world will find a home in any political party, no matter what the names of those parties may be. All of that was lost on the producers of this *Hard Times*. They went so far as to have Gradgrind's old pupil-turned-traitor, Bitzer, throw the word "conservative" in the old man's face. That word is not to be found in the text. Gradgrind is not old-fashioned. He is newfangled.

What is found in the text, though, are a lot of things that a genuine conservative would hold dear. Foremost among them is an abiding religious faith, shining through the characters who redeem those who would otherwise die in their sins, their folly, and their despair. That faith pierces through the muddle of a grim and heartless world, revealing the triviality and ineffectuality of all those systems for man's reform which forget that man is man and not a machine; that he has a soul, capable of grandeur and pettiness, virtue and the depths of vice. The actors and actresses hobbled through the script like people asked to walk around all day in unfamiliar clothes. Which, of course, they were. Maybe a couple of them should have applied for a job in my old department too.

## Clear Your Mind of Cant

One of the strange features of Unreal City is a simultaneous obsession with language, and a general refusal to acknowledge what language is for. A sane person understands that reality comes first, and language later; language is in the service of reality. I do not mean that language has no influence upon what we will see or conceive. But the thing is primary, not our concepts about the thing. Let me give an example. One of the canards I have heard for many years is that the Inuit people, living on the delta of the Mackenzie River, have twelve or twenty different words for snow. That is by way of showing how our sense of reality depends upon the language we use to describe it. I believe, however, that the Inuit, whose lives sometimes depend upon their being able to tell the difference between powder and granular snow and sleet, will have a broader variety of words to use to name the white stuff, because in fact they are describing different things, and the differences are sometimes an urgent matter.

The reality is that sleet is not powder. Why, we ourselves do not merely say "snow".

We want to believe that *our words* can alter reality: we want to believe that we can, by linguistic magic, negate the Word through whom all things were made, and the things themselves. "You shall be as gods", said the serpent (Gen 3:5).[5] Hence the battle in our day is theological, whether we wish to admit it or not. If a man claims to be a woman, which he can never be, and demands to be addressed as such, he is not merely asking for right etiquette. He is demanding that we enter his delusion, or his lie. It is not true. He is demanding that believers in God fall in worship of an idol. Some idols are hideous, like Moloch, and some are beautiful, like Dionysus. The Hebrew prophets did not care. They did not condemn the idols for their style. They condemned them for being *false*. We have names for people who accustom themselves to speaking what they know to be untrue. We call them scoundrels or cowards. That a certain realm of our lives—the technological—is held mostly immune from our falsehoods does not necessarily make things better. We are scoundrels and cowards, with airplanes, computers, and bombs.

After a while, the habit of speaking falsely renders us incapable even of recognizing that we are doing so. It is a danger against which men have always had to guard. I am thinking here of a famous passage in James Boswell's brilliant biography, *The Life of Johnson*. Doctor Johnson, a bluff man who had in his youth experienced plenty of suffering and privation, and who was, as we would recognize now, beset with severe neurological pathologies, was not one to be de-

---

[5] All Scripture quotations are from the King James Version unless otherwise noted.

ceived by the trite, the merely pleasant, or the self-deceptive. So he called his friend Boswell out for speaking cant, when Boswell expressed his vexation at the Whigs in Parliament. Johnson was a true-blue Tory and assured Boswell that he would have greatly liked to "knock[ ] the factious dogs on the head", but he was not *vexed*. For "vexed", in our parlance today, read "offended".

"I declare, Sir," said Boswell, "upon my honor, I did imagine that I was vexed, and took a pride in it; but it was, perhaps, cant; for I own I neither ate less, nor slept less."

Here I will note that the touchy in our time neither eat less nor lose any sleep but are quite ferociously gleeful when they catch someone in a supposed offense against their sensibilities. And in that fierce glee they never trouble to address the question of truth. They are too busy being proud of themselves, as Boswell admitted he had been.

"My dear friend," replied the good Doctor,

> clear your mind of cant. You may talk as other people do: you may say to a man, "Sir, I am your most humble servant." You are not his most humble servant. You may say, "These are sad times; it is a melancholy thing to be reserved to such times." You don't mind the times. You tell a man, "I am sorry you had such bad weather the last day of your journey, and were so much wet." You don't care sixpence whether he was wet or dry. You may talk in this manner; it is a mode of talking in Society: but don't think foolishly.[6]

Almost all of our talk about social matters is foolish. Its mode is that of the advertiser, the huckster, the politician. It has set its roots in our schools, as I have said.

[6] James Boswell, *The Life of Samuel Johnson* (New York: Penguin Books, 2008), 884–85.

I once attended, under duress, a seminar on the new-and-improved methods of education to which students in Rhode Island would be subject. The three sixtyish ladies who hosted it were pleasant enough. They might have put on a fine ice cream social. They would have been at home on the veranda, pouring lemonade. But underneath their thickets of Educanto it was all the same old flight from content, from memory, from wonder, and from truth. I could not get into the specifics of it, because there were no specifics. It was cant, "a mode of talking in Society", now disastrously transferred into the curriculum and made its centerpiece. Much of the current fad in elementary and secondary education, the so-called Common Core, is just the same wearisome flight from wonder and beauty as Mr. Gradgrind forced upon the helpless young people in his school in Coketown. It is merely dressed up in advertising rather than smudged and smeared with the smoke of burning coal. "Core", for instance, suggests a heart; but there is no heart.

What really struck me about our meeting that day was not the presentation. As far as that went, my low expectations turned out to be optimistic. It was instead the discussion by the college professors in the room, most of whom happened to be old-fashioned scholars in the pursuit of truth. We knew we were looking at a terrible mess, yet we could not openly say why. The cant, you see, went both ways. We could say nothing deeply honest about a system that reliably turns children of above-average intelligence into large adolescents who cannot parse a single sentence not written by Dr. Seuss. We were tongue-tied by an all-invading etiquette, transferred from the tea table where it belongs, where for the sake of digestion and affability certain subjects are not brought up, to education—or politics, or religion. The arena of intellectual combat was shut down. What is left may be nice or it may be nasty, as at a tea table; but it is not free, and it is not honest.

The *agon*, the arena of combat, is no more. In 1982, Walter Ong, S.J., in *Orality and Literacy*, noted that in American colleges the masculine virtue of courage and free fighting in the pursuit of truth was being set aside in favor of the expression of feelings and the championing of political ideals. That was a long time ago. We are no more talking about a patient burdened with a parasitic disease. We are talking about an enormous parasite that has engulfed what used to be a patient.

How many are the things we cannot discuss now, in the public arena, without being ruled by that "mode of talking in Society"! The most frequented building in the native Micmac village near to our summer home in Canada is a casino. In it, working-class men drain their salaries away and ruin their families. May I say that it is a dreadful thing to visit upon the natives, who need to recover the old virtues that made for stable family life, led by strong men and not overgrown boys? No, I may not, not without being accused of wicked intent.

The five-alarm fire of unreality that is the "transgender" movement is not, as is sometimes alleged, misogynist. It is just the overheating and the extension of the four-alarm fire of unreality that was feminism to begin with. Feminism says that women and men are not made for one another, and therefore their interests are separable. That is a lie. Transgenderism agrees with the lie and adds that a woman can be made into a man, or vice versa, or perhaps back and forth by turns, as happened to Tiresias of old. The feminists said that the differences between the sexes were minimal and that they were confined to the region of plumbing. The only thing that a male soldier could do that a female soldier could not do, said one of the more obnoxious and ungrateful of the latter, was to urinate through a hole in a fence. Those who are all for the alteration of genders agree, except now they say that in fact some women *can* urinate through a hole in the fence, namely those men who "feel" they are women but who do not go so far as to make geldings of themselves.

(Dear reader, if you should happen upon these words a thousand years from now, know that our initial sin of denying the goodness of male and female first became a denial of their very existence, and then an affirmation that they might be whatever we imagined them to be. It is as mad as if some people had insisted on being transspecial, really cats in semihuman form. And in fact some people did just that.)

It is a plain truth that many of our social problems would fade away if we returned to sexual expectations that prevailed when my father first courted my mother. When people say that members of certain groups among us suffer because of the scorn they meet from the socially "privileged", by way of arguing against what I have just said, I confess to wondering whether they themselves believe what they say. For if it were true that a Cherokee, for example, is at birth three steps behind in the race for material success, then *all the more does he require the severe and masculine virtues*, of courage, self-denial, farsightedness, and wisdom in governing his household. The rich can afford their cant and their easy vices. They can feed on macaroons. The poor cannot. They need the solid meat of truth and virtue.

But you must not talk about women, period. You must not talk about boys, and the shabby neglect they suffer. You must not talk about Other Religions. You must not talk about Indigenous Peoples. You must not talk about the failings of democracy. You must not talk about what is probably an irreversible decline, accelerated by technology, in our ability to read and think. You must not don the gloves to spar about—about donning the gloves to spar. All is the cant of a pernicious etiquette. Extend your pinkies, everybody. Right, left, or center, "political correctness" is misnamed. It abolishes the arena of the polis.

## Oh, for the Skeptics of Old!

"Skeptic", wrote Pascal, thinking Descartes, or that incarnation of the urbane, Michel de Montaigne, whom he admired and detested at once. "Skeptic, for obstinate."[7]

I could dearly wish for the skeptics of old, who demanded reason, evidence, and demonstration. Such a one was the amiable MacPhee, in C. S. Lewis' novel *That Hideous Strength*. He was welcome among the believers, both for the goodness of his heart and for his staid insistence upon what he could be shown was the *truth*. I am reminded also of Lewis' character Emeth, in *The Last Battle*. He is a devotee of the false god Tash, but he follows the natural law as well as he can, by his best lights, so that the devotion he thinks he pays to Tash, he actually pays to Aslan, Lewis' allegory for the true and only Son of God. When Emeth asks Aslan whether he will accept his misdirected devotion because he and Tash are similar, Aslan replies that it is precisely because they are irreconcilably *different* that the true worship cannot be paid to Tash. It does not stick.

The name Emeth, as Lewis knew, means "truth" in Hebrew. It is related to the word "amen", and it suggests something weighty, dependable, like a rock. You need not fear when you have the Rock of Ages to lean upon.

[7] Blaise Pascal, *Pensées*, trans. W. F. Trotter (New York: Random House, 1941).

I find that the rock of the Christian faith permits a man to retain a healthy skepticism about all things that the faith does not decide upon. Chesterton noted it also. He said that when he became a Catholic, he had to accept the tenets of the Nicene Creed, but that on almost everything that was in the political hurly-burly of the time, the Church lent him a remarkable liberty. By contrast, many are the things, undemonstrated, or undemonstrable, or flatly false, that the unbeliever must accept, lest he be banished from polite society or lose his job.

Because truth and not what is politically expedient is the rock of my salvation, I may remain skeptical, for example, about whether the earth is warming to a dangerous degree, whether democracy is the finest form of government man has invented, or whether compulsory schooling has spread knowledge or stupidity. I am in the arena and have girt up my loins. At me then, with your arguments. Not your feelings, which are of no consequence.

We might think that if you lose your faith in God, you will probably have no faith in anything else, either. It is not so. Man is made for faith: he is *homo credens*. If he does not believe in God, he will turn straightaway to some idol, a stock or stone, himself, the state, sex—something stupid, salacious, or malignant, like a cancer. Man without faith becomes *credulous*.

From *The Most of Malcolm Muggeridge*, a collection of essays printed in paperback in 1969, before the author's conversion to Christianity, comes this superb analysis of mass man's proneness to accepting anything, no matter how absurd. I should not accuse mass man so harshly without noting, again, that he is usually preceded in parade by the self-styled intellectuals. Ordinary people are seldom as imaginatively stupid as are the intelligentsia. In any case, Muggeridge is concluding an article on the hyping of an Air Force pilot named Claude Eatherly into a pacifist saint.

The story that the purveyors of mendacity, that is, newspapers, radio, television, and the silver screen, wanted to believe and wanted everybody else to believe was that Mr. Eatherly was a distinguished soldier so sickened by his part in the bombing of Hiroshima that he turned to a life of crime, in the fashion of the modern martyr who witnesses to the truth by killing *other people*. Eatherly wanted to cause people to notice and listen. The truth turned out to be a good deal more edifying, if you really want to learn about the tangles of that jungle called the heart of man, wicked from his youth.

Eatherly was annoyed at *not* having played a bigger part in Hiroshima, or not being recognized for his role. He then tried his hardest to be assigned to the experimental bombing at Bikini Atoll. He cheated on the exam and was tossed out of the service with an honorable discharge. Then he went home to his wife and got involved in a criminal plot to bomb Havana. He drank a lot, drifted into crime, and was basically a worthless lout, in and out of mental wards and prison. There he was visited by a newspaper reporter, who stretched his story a wee bit, and then someone else came along and stretched it some more, and the rest, alas, is what we call history. Here is Muggeridge's conclusion:

> It has long been my opinion that the most appropriate name for the times in which we live would be the Age of Credulity. . . . Science (the very word has undergone a singular distortion; meaning originally a condition of knowing, it has come to signify particular branches of knowledge), which purports to inculcate skepticism, has

surrendered the human mind to a degree of absurdity which
would have astounded a medieval scholar and made an
African witch doctor green with envy.

In the now little read short stories of O. Henry there
are two con men—Jeff Peters and Andy Tucker—who regard it as unethical to sell gold bricks to farmers because it
is too easy. Had these two worthies had the advantage and
pleasure of reading . . . *The Hiroshima Pilot*, they would
have realized that, compared with the fine flower of our
Western intelligentsia, farmers are a hard sell.[8]

I'll sign on to that.

Let's see, now. I was a boy once, and have watched children playing all my life long. I was taught that boys and girls
are different, in ways that I had come to find sometimes frus-
trating but usually delightful, and that bit of folksy wisdom
jibed with what I saw of them. But now I am supposed to
believe that in every culture known to man, at every stage of
technological development, and usually quite independent
of one another, boys invent rough games, organize themselves into teams or gangs, and worship heroes, and this is
*all* a matter of cultural conditioning and could be completely
otherwise; but when some grown man wants to dress up as
a bride and saunter down the aisle with another grown man,
and sow seed where seed don't go, now *that* is natural, nay,
absolutely determined by the jeans, I mean genes. Call me
a skeptic.

When I was a boy, people used to call it a tragedy if a
child lost his mother or father by death or divorce. That
seemed right to me; I knew a couple of those kids. But one
of my former colleagues, a nominal Catholic, unmarried,
adopted a healthy little boy to raise as her own, without a

[8] Malcolm Muggeridge, *The Most of Malcolm Muggeridge* (New York: Simon and Schuster, 1969), 249–50.

father. I was supposed to believe that this was a wonderful thing. I was supposed to join the party. Call me a skeptic.

I cannot believe that our children of divorce and of shacking up are just fine, not hurt by it, no, not a bit. It would be tedious for me to recount what divorce and shacking up have done to the families of five or six of our closest friends, but I am supposed to ignore all that and believe, with a toss of the head, that marriage, or keeping your vows, would have been worse. I have observed, closely, marriages that were terrible; and I have seen bad husbands and wives grow even worse because of the possibility of divorce. I have seen them go on and make other people's lives miserable, like free radicals ranging through the body. I am supposed to ignore it and believe, just believe.

I believe in God, the Father, the Almighty, Creator of heaven and earth. That belief is reasonable. I can argue for it. I have done so. A corollary of that belief is a trust in the reality and intelligibility and integrity of created things. I like very much what Chesterton wanted to call Saint Thomas Aquinas: Saint Thomas of the Creation, for just that rock-steady trust in what is. So long as you keep your hold on that first tenet of the Creed—and a "tenet" is literally what you grab hold of, like a mountain climber clasping a good firm outcropping of stone—you will not fall into the crevasse of unreality.

Now think of the condition of young people who attend our public schools and universities. They reach for the rock, as they must, as they were created to do, and grasp nothing but air.

# 2

# The Body Unreal

In 1859 Charles Darwin burst upon the world with his work, *The Origin of Species*, wherein he posited his theory of the common ancestry of all forms of life, and their branching out into our current broad variety of species, by means of small adaptive or maladaptive changes, sifted out for further reproduction by the urgencies of survival. His theory has come to be named "evolution", though Darwin himself did not originate the term. One of the ironies of the title of his book, an irony that Darwin himself was aware of, is that his theory would tend to dissolve the term "species".

Étienne Gilson noted as much in *From Aristotle to Darwin and Back Again* (1971). Aristotle, the philosopher with the mind of a biologist, saw final causality or purpose in the features of living things, and formal cause, that is, fundamental principles of structure, in the features and their interrelationships. A dog is not a dog because of the batch of matter that makes him up, since that matter is subject to continual change. He is also not a dog, if we are to trust Darwin, merely because his sire and his dam were dogs. He is a dog, said Aristotle, because of the canine organization of his organs—his form; and his form is the sort of thing that tends to its full realization or end in the health of an adult dog, capable of reproducing after his kind.

It is my object here not to argue about evolution but

rather to notice how the *idea* has spread, like a fungus, to an area where it does not belong. In the old way of looking at things, by what has been called the *philosophia perennis*, the philosophy that does not go out of date with the years, we see that a dog is a dog and not a cat, and that fact determines our language. The species are real. The statement "I see the dog", understood with its full epistemological and ontological import, comes near in our time to the defiant witness that the martyrs of old gave, when they confessed Christ before pagans who hated and feared them and thirsted for their blood. Whether from dogs in general may be born, fifty thousand years hence, a creature that is not a dog, I do not know. I do know that for all purposes in the present, the species are what they are. They are in fact *specific*. They exist in a taxonomy of being, as is suggested by the sacred author, who says that God created them *according to their kinds* (Gen 1:25).

The *kind* is real. A dog is not a dog along a spectrum ranging from dog to cat. There is no such spectrum. It is one of the strange features of Darwinian theory, that we are to believe in tiny, even infinitesimal, increments from one kind of beast to another over time, while witnessing no such infinitesimal increments from one kind of beast to another at any one time. Indeed, if we turn to chemistry, we find not a spectrum of atoms but highly specific kinds, with specific features and properties. There is no such thing as an atom that is half sodium and half manganese. Sodium is sodium, and manganese is manganese.

Yet what I will call "spectral" thinking has overtaken taxonomy. The kinds of things vanish, as if our division of living creatures into dogs and cats and others were merely arbitrary. We simply cordon off, with movable boundaries, what shall be called "dog" and what shall be called "cat".

This is the old philosophy called nominalism. It is an attempt, not to solve the question of when a thing belongs to this kind rather than that, but to evade it.

"I am her corrupter of words", says the clown Feste, referring to his self-deceived mistress, the Lady Olivia.[1] The first step along the way to such corruption is to deny that words refer to stable things in reality. *Nomina sunt consequentia rerum*, went the old medieval wisdom: Names are consequent upon the things they name. We do not have to believe that man sees a dog and, *ping*, a bell chimes in his head, and he thinks of a word fit for it. The sheer variety of words in the languages of the world rules that out. What we mean instead is what I have been insisting upon throughout. Adam names the beasts and in naming them seeks to dis-cover, to un-veil, some real feature of their being. That means that they have real features to recognize and to name. The world is given to us, as it was given to Adam. Names should reveal, not conceal. The beginning of wisdom, said Confucius, is to call things by their proper names.

The French philosophical fad called "deconstruction", harping on a single loose string, made the illegitimate move from noticing the variety of words we use to name things, to suggesting that there were no stable realities to name. If you believe that there are stable realities, they said, giving away their true animus, you are "logocentric", by which they meant not that you were fascinated with words (Greek *logoi*) but that you were somewhere in the camp of the *Logos*, the Word by whom, as Christians believe, all things were made. Antipatriarchal feminists, humorless creatures with no sense of absurdity, would go on to say that if you

---

[1] William Shakespeare, *Twelfth Night*, ed. M. M. Mahood (New York: Penguin Books, 1968), act 3, scene 1, lines 34–35.

insist upon the primacy of real things, you are *phallocentric*. If you can get through the logorrhea of both the deconstructionists and their bedfellows the feminists, you see both a carelessness with language and a disdain for the world and the Word that made it.

I will have more to say about the *Word* that was with God in the beginning and that was God. It may seem odd, meanwhile, that a chapter about *bodies* should begin with a discussion of *words*. But the unreality of the "transgender" movement, set ablaze by the wildfire of the sexual revolution generally, depends for its existence upon the supposition that realities depend upon words, so that whoever controls the language controls the universe. It is as if we could say "same-sex marriage", and hey presto, there would be such a thing, or as if a man could declare himself to be a woman, and so it is. It is as if we were gods, as he who was a liar and a murderer from the beginning promised us.

We are not, as the estimable Robert George reminds us, specters in a machine, "selves", detachable from the body, with the liberty to fashion ourselves along a spectrum of choices as we please. That is not what a human being is. Think again of dogs. My dog Jasper is not a dog-self, accidentally located within a canine body. He is also not simply reducible to his body. When he dies, the body will still be there for a while, but the dog will not. No one supposes that you can create an electronic file with my dog's memories and instincts and habits, and activate a robot with it, and that will "be" Jasper. The dog is the whole creature, body and dog-form together. Man, possessed of an immaterial soul—immaterial and, as not only Christians believe, immortal—is the whole creature, body and soul together, a unity. Thus, the promise to us is not that disembodied souls will live on forever but that, to quote the poet Tasso,

soul and body shall again unite
in Godlike immortality and light.[2]

"We shall be like him", says the apostle John, thinking
of the resurrection of the flesh, and "we shall see him as he
is" (1 Jn 3:2). As he is: the resurrected Lord, in the glorified
flesh. The painter Caravaggio made the point most power-
fully and indeed disturbingly, when the risen Christ, with
calm patience, guides the finger of the doubting Thomas
beneath the flesh of the wound in his side, and you can see
the bulge of Thomas' fingertip from within.

## Prickly-Gorse and Finicky-Broom

All human cultures have had to embrace reality to survive.
That includes the reality of male and female bodies.

In *The Horse of Pride: Life in a Breton Village* (1978), the
stage actor and Breton cultural conservator Pierre-Jakez
Hélias writes about what it was like to grow up on the foggy,
rainy peninsula of Brittany before the Second World War.
He is writing long after it has come to him with the weight of
nostalgia that that way of life—or, more accurately, that dis-
tinctive Breton culture—had nearly disappeared. He mourns
this impoverishment, not because he thought that the old
ways were all wise and good, all sweetness and light. His
chapter-long description of what happens when someone
dies is a fascinating study in charity and pride, generosity
and selfishness. Who comes to pay respects to the body?
Where do the people sit, and who gets to sit where? If you
are kin but you live far away, and you cannot afford to leave

---

[2] Torquato Tasso, *Jerusalem Delivered*, trans. Anthony M. Esolen (Baltimore: Johns Hopkins University Press, 2000), canto 8, stanza 30, lines 7–8,
p. 165.

your farm, what do you do? Who cleans the corpse if it is a man, and who does it if it is a woman? Who is that odd fellow showing up before the priest, singing out prayers of his own half-wild devising?

Hélias mourns its loss, just as we would mourn a particular friend—*this* man here, this Ed with the big ears, or this Joe who never could turn down a bottle of gin; because it was a good thing to live at the same time and in the same place as this Ed or this Joe, and now the old slob is gone, and we are the poorer for it.

There is a lot of humor too in the book, some of it lost on the B-minus sociology student who evidently owned my copy before I did. When the author was a little boy, his grandfather, one of those big-shouldered shambling grandfatherly sorts who knows all things and says some of them, explained to him the difference between the sexes. "Girls are like broom, and boys are like gorse," he said. The broom, he explained, flowers all spring and summer and has long slender delicate branches that sway in the wind. Girls are like that, he said, and that is why they sweep the broom in the house. Boys, he went on, are hard and spiny like the gorse bush. You cannot easily grab them without getting a thorn in your hand. They do not bloom for long, but they are tough, and they stay outdoors, and they brave the elements. So, of course, when the lad and his sister were on the outs with one another, she would call him prickly-gorse, and he would call her finicky-broom, and each thought it was good to be gorse or broom and silly to be the other.[3] Which was, when you think of it, healthy enough, and exactly right. My B-minus sociology student, misunderstand-

---

[3] Pierre-Jakez Hélias, *The Horse of Pride: Life in a Breton Village*, trans. June Guicharnaud (New Haven: Yale University Press, 1978), pp. 56–57.

ing the anecdote and evidently never having had to do any work to raise calluses all over the hands, wrote at the top of the page, "Gender dichotomy very strict."

Well, I doubt a Breton woman would have looked twice at a young man who said to her, "I should like to spend most of the day in the house cooking and knitting. You can tend the animals, plow the fields, and chop down trees." The point is that a way of life comes to be what it is because it works—and more than that, because people fall in love with it. It becomes theirs, as the land is theirs. It is important to assert that this way of life I am talking about is not describable by mere statistics. It is a culture, embracing every single person living within it, and all of them together in their families and clans and parishes. Now it may be that the culture that Hélias describes could not possibly survive the world war. For cultures, like Ed and Joe, go the way of all flesh; they are born and they flower, they age and they die. But we ought to shed a tear for them when they die, as we would shed a tear for Ed or Joe. And we should hope that if a culture must die, it would be succeeded by another culture, just as, though Ed may no longer be with us, his grandson Matty is, and right now is standing on the fencepost teasing the dog with a bicycle horn.

Without a *modus vivendi* between the sexes, you can bid farewell to any chance for a culture, and you will not get that *modus vivendi* if you do not raise boys to be men. And you cannot do that unless you pay close and appreciative attention to the needs and the realities of the male body.

The Boy Scouts used to do that. I have several issues of their magazine, *Boys' Life*, from its earliest years of publication in the United States, and the issues are filled with stories of adventure, tales of pranks, a pep talk from a minister, and instructions on building, bird watching, fishing, camping, and other outdoor activities. The idea was that the manhood of a nation must be built up from its boyhood. That idea was shared by everyone across all religious and political divisions. It was like agreeing that houses ought to be warm and dry, and food nutritious and plentiful, and clothing decent and attractive. In no case did people believe that you could have a stable society without stable homes, or stable homes without stable marriages, or stable marriages without upstanding men and women. And you can only get the men from the boys.

The Boy Scouts in the United States are declaring bankruptcy. The Scouts—I mean the boys and not the organization—were betrayed by the pelvic Left, for whom sexual individualism, that is, a display and sale of self that is a craven surrender to what the old Left saw as the evils of an untrammeled market, is the lone "liberty" worth defending. The Scouts were betrayed by the craven quasi Left, known as the Right, who were at best meek in their defense. The Scouts were persecuted by activists, including some from the now wholly pelvic Girl Scouts of America, who hated what was good and natural about the boys' organization. The Boy Scouts had maintained their requirement that the boy acknowledge God and obey him, and they had maintained a perfectly sensible prohibition against males among their number who would look upon boys as objects of sexual delight. Then they caved in, all on their own. Having given up on sexual reality, they could no longer see the very object for which the organization was invented. They had fallen into ignorance of boys.

It should not have been so. Several years ago I read an article in the *Washington Post* about eleven boys from a single Boy Scout troop who had all made Eagle Scout together, a feat that Scout leaders thought might be unprecedented in the organization's history. The boys, who called themselves the Viking Patrol, were initially a bunch of whiners and losers—"ninnies", as one of the leaders called them—lying down in the middle of the trail along one of their first hikes, a gentle three-miler. Women do not call girls "ninnies", though perhaps they should, once in a while. Men call boys a lot worse things than that, and can do it right, with love, to build the boys up.

The article did not give too many details about what transformed them, but a couple of things stood out. The leaders responded to the boys' sissiness by making things *more* difficult for them, not easier. Think of the boy-body, needing work. The turning point came when, on a hike in Alaska, the boys did not want to pitch their tents, did not want to hang their food up so as not to attract bears, and did not want to set up their latrines. So the leaders left them to themselves. The result was that they did organize themselves after all. They formed a *team*, the essential male group, and got the jobs done.

After that, they were on their way. The article mentions, without delving into it, that a couple of the leaders were ex-military men; and it does seem that the leaders had especial fondness for rugged hikes, hunting, and mechanics. They did not have the boys do macramé. And yet, because the boys were amongst themselves, and did not have to care what anybody looking over their shoulder would think, they seem to have grown interested in things gentler than shooting moose: planting butterfly bushes, for example, or talking about Bergman films. For that is one of the mysteries of a boy's life that is hidden in plain sight. Among boys alone, you do not have to pitch yourself into a caricature of boyhood. You need not exaggerate your masculinity to show off in front of girls, to distinguish yourself from them, and to put the lesser boys in their place. None of that happens. Roosevelt Grier did needlepoint. Rosey Grier was an offensive lineman for the New York Giants and the Los Angeles Rams. Rosey Grier was six feet five and weighed nearly three hundred pounds; and they called him Rosey.

The *Post* did not sniff in contempt at the achievements of the boys, though there was the requisite (and discouraging) allusion to the precipitous fall in Boy Scout membership, from 4.3 million in 1970 to 2.9 million in 2006, a drop only partly explained by demographics. And the article did allude to the only press the Boy Scouts now get—namely, when the organization has to divert many millions of its dollars from hikes, canoe trips, table saws, and chartered buses, to lawyers to help them fend off plaintiffs of various sorts who detest what the organization is about, because they are not fond of the creatures whom the organization is dedicated to help.

There was a lot to read between the lines in the *Post* article. It was clear, even from the pretty sketchy story, that the boys developed both personally and intellectually; and I do not think that the development was attributable to a couple of years of growing taller. I teach nineteen-year-olds for a living, after all. You can hardly say it without inviting a chorus of jeers, but the history of the human race does not show that boys, after a certain age, develop their full intellectual potential, or anything close to it, under the primary tutelage of women. That does not mean that they cannot have some women as teachers. I know plenty of women who make fine teachers of young men. What these women all have in common, though, is a deep appreciation for them as young *men*, and not just as generically young *people*. And they would also be the last women to claim that the young men could get *everything* they needed from them. My opinions in this regard have only gotten stronger as women have shown less and less consideration for the needs of the boy or the young man, less willingness to forgive his waywardness, and less grateful for his gifts.

Another politically incorrect truth that the account illustrates is that, for the male, difficulty, whether intellectual or physical, brings hope; there are bruises that feel good because they are the bruises of a real life, a real struggle. This is again reality speaking. Bones grow by bruising. I make no claim about young women here, except that I do not think that they *die inside* without some arena, some *agon*, where you can win or lose, but at least lose fighting. Girls do not organize themselves for the great sweaty fight. But for the boy, with his thicker skin (males possess an extra layer of it), his more active metabolism, his more highly oxygenated blood, and his *angularity*, a life without the creativity of the fight is a kind of death. There is a bitterness in the easy, the silly, the pointless, and it is all the more dispiriting when it is combined, as it is in a lot of the school assignments I have seen, with imbecilic drudgery.

A boy is that odd creature who, if he cannot clear the low bar, needs to have it raised higher. But that counterintuitive challenge can be issued only under certain circumstances, by people who are motivated by love and who know what they are doing. Usually that means you need a gang of boys, not just one, and a leader who knows more about them than he can even articulate, because he was once one of them. There are all kinds of lessons here too for attracting more young men to the ordained ministry.

One more point. I think here of Edmund Burke's comment that there is nothing colder than the heart of a confirmed "metaphysical" politician. That heart is wickeder than the passions of men because it is closer to that unmixed intellectual evil that dwells below, as the Florentine traveler would have it, locked in ice. To subject children of either sex to the demands of a political ideology is wicked. Let us recall the order of things. All economy is or ought to be for the welfare of the family; the family is not something to be experimented upon, like an amphibian in formaldehyde, or colonized by our supposed betters in the elites of media, education, and politics. Let them instead doff their hats and bow before the reality. In the order of human goods upon this earth, the family, cradle of all relationships and, as Pope Leo XIII acutely observes in *Rerum novarum*, anterior to all states, is primary. All other things come second.

If only some self-styled liberal could have set aside the unreal metaphysics of the Left and noticed, as a plain matter of fact, that the Boy Scouts used to *work*, such a man could have then said, to those who would harry all such organizations out of existence, "Leave them alone. Boys are what they are, and let us thank God for it. We must care about one thing and that alone: to save as many boys as I can from the gangs, the gutters, and the grave. Let us have results."

## Return to the Body

I must here insist that the boy's nature is in concord with the boy's body, and the girl's nature is in concord with the girl's body. That does not mean that all boys will enjoy rough play. Sometimes there is a peculiarity in the nervous system that rules it out. It does not mean that all boys will want to lie underneath the chassis of a car, investigating things. Our interests are varied. It does not mean that all girls will like to play with dolls, practicing as children what they must do as mothers. The chances and changes of human existence can cause us to lean in any number of directions. But the natures remain, as do the bodies. And both are good and necessary.

Sometimes whole societies make long forays into madness, but such a situation cannot endure, and people return to something like sanity. Consider again this business of a "transgender" movement. There are people of either sex who believe that they are really members of the other. How they can know this, no one says. It is a mere feeling, usually a feeling of intense dissatisfaction or disgust with one's own sex and one's body. It is like anorexia in that regard: as when young women who are nothing but skin and bones feel they are fat and see only fat, and they starve themselves to get rid of what does not exist.

Adults in the grip of this sexual delusion are now encouraging children to join them. They are subjecting the children to irreversible mutilation of the body, castrating little boys and performing mastectomies on teenage girls, to live a fantasy, a pretense. For there are well over six thousand physical differences between males and females, and all the surgeries can do is to mimic some appearance of the opposite sex, such as make chin hair grow on females or swell the breasts of males with fat. Some males have themselves castrated and then ask surgeons to trowel out a cavity in the crotch to mimic a vagina. Some females have the pin-the-tail operation, to be fitted out with a mock *membrum virile.* The whole movement is ghastly.

The unreality of it all comes home whenever a boy or a man, declaring himself, with or without mutilation, to be female, competes in a sport against girls or women. The results have been broken bones and humiliation for the females. For the only way that female sports can exist is by the

exclusion of males. In any large human group, barring constitutional frailty, if we assume that all the young people are
healthy and that they are at the peak of their physical powers
—as would be the case by natural effects in any society in
which people must do hard physical work, and as would be
the case, we hope, after basic training for the army—it is not
just that the young men will be generally stronger than the
young women. For all practical purposes, *all* the young men
will be stronger than *all* the young women. There will be
no overlap. No mother of a seventeen-year-old boy, if the
boy does plenty of labor outdoors, will be stronger than
her son. It will not be close. He has probably already sur-
passed her by age fourteen. As for his father—he will not be
stronger than his father for a long time to come, if the old
man is in good health. But nobody in charge of our schools
has dared to say the obvious, that the aim to change one's
sex is madness. That is just as nobody in our churches has
dared to say the obvious, that if men are bound to protect
women and children, it is a glaring contradiction to place
women in harm's way, in the battlefield, regardless of their
inclinations. Nobody dares to consider what happens to a
good man inside when he must stand beside a female soldier
about to be torn to pieces and do nothing for her beyond
what he would do for a man. But bodies are what they are.
Feelings do not change facts. But contradictions cause people to go badly wrong. Unreason hurts.

I recently heard from a professor of chemistry who told
me that he had gotten into trouble with his female students
for "misogyny". His crime was realism, thus. He had mentioned in class that he enjoyed going hunting in the Blue
Ridge Mountains of Virginia for pheasant, woodcock, and
grouse. To that end he bought and trained a bird dog. Was it
a boy dog or a girl dog? A girl dog, he replied. He explained

that the female dogs of that breed were more "biddable" and that they would be more likely to return with the quarry intact, while the male dogs would be more likely to mangle it and gobble some of it first, spoiling it. That was it, that was all.

In speaking about this incident, I heard from another man, a former professor of art. His job was to teach anatomical drawing, and he got into trouble when he tried to correct the work of some students who could not draw the male and female bodies correctly. He tried to explain the difference between the male pelvis and the female pelvis, in width and in how the bones open out. When he asked a female art professor to let him know how he might talk about such things without giving offense, she replied that anatomy was a male construct and that art students, especially the feminists, need have nothing to do with it. He told me that he soon left that line of work. Who knows how many artists will have had their talents thwarted by such political nonsense? Leonardo could draw a human body. These artists cannot. Leonardo studied anatomy, with painstaking exactitude. These artists have not. Hence, they will draw forms that will be like sagging bridges. Sane people, when we have sane people again, will notice it and evaluate the work accordingly. But living in Unreal has made it hard for us to imagine anything else.

And the nonsense is everywhere.

Not so long ago I warned, in a book called *Defending Marriage: Ten Arguments for Sanity* (2014), that the social acceptance in the United States of the biological and anthropological impossibility of same-sex marriage, or rather same-sex mirage, would visit a crisis of identity upon every child in the land, most especially upon those children who, through no fault of their own, were particularly vulnerable. I was thinking of boys growing up without a father in the home, who cannot model themselves after a man who loves them and who shows them, mostly by quiet example, what a man is, how a good man treats women, and how a man stands alongside other men in getting important or difficult or dangerous things done. I had thought, at the time, that the main objection would be that such a crisis of identity, a very bad thing, would probably not occur, because the natures of individual boys would rule. In other words, I had thought that the objection would depend upon an irresponsible and careless optimism.

I see now that there is no objection to the crisis at all: it is *welcomed*. It is a fad now, among librarians and teachers, to have Drag Queen Story Hour, so that toddlers and boys and girls in the period of what ought to be their sexual latency can have the confusion thrust upon them, with cookies and sugary drinks and smiles all around. What would have been considered, only a few years ago, as degenerate, and as corrupting the morals of minors, is now celebrated, and anyone who opposes it is labeled a hater—a very bad man.

"But all they are doing is reading stories", someone may say. If it were only so, what is the point of dressing as a member of the opposite sex? Can a man not read *Winnie-the-Pooh* unless he puts on a skirt? Can a man not recite *The Grinch Who Stole Christmas* without mascara and lipstick? No, the whole point is to indoctrinate little children, who have not the slightest idea what is really going on, in sexual behavior that is against their nature and that will make the fulfillment of their nature harder to attain. For how will a drag queen help a little boy learn to become a man, so that he can marry a woman and have children? The drag queen is there rather as misdirection. We do not want to encourage the little boy to become a man. We do not want the normal and natural. We want the abnormal and perverse. It is only the abnormal and perverse that can arouse a people who are weary of old reliable reality—as is shown at the end of the indecent but bitterly honest movie *Carnal Knowledge* (1971), wherein the slob of a hero is so burned out by years of sexual sin that he can no longer perform the normal function of a man with a woman.

So the drag queen—a ghastly fellow in a town near us, calling himself, with bawdy suggestion, Monique Toosoon—is there not for the children but for himself. He does not serve their good. Their good is sacrificed to his unreality. That is what I have called the moral structure of pedophilia, and it is everywhere to be found in our time. The welfare of children is subordinated to the sexual gratification of adults. When more than half our children will experience what it is like to lack either a father or a mother in the home, what else can we say?

"But what is the difference between a man pretending to be a woman, and any kind of acting? If a man can pretend to be King George, why can he not pretend to be Queen Victoria?" Well . . . is that what is going on? Not even a child, says Philip Sidney, thinks that the stage is Thebes just because the actors say so. The poet does not lie, because he does not affirm: it is only play. But that is not what the drag queen is doing. He is not analogous to Raymond Massey playing Abraham Lincoln, or Charlton Heston playing Michelangelo. He is analogous to a self-described witch who believes that she can cast spells. If a witch puts on a show about witchcraft for children, she is not acting. The drag queen does not say, "Hey, kids, I'm a man acting as a woman—let's have a laugh at how silly I can be!" He takes the whole thing seriously. In his mind, *he is a queen*. He has no intention of doffing the costume and then acting the part of Sherman at Savannah. His aim is not to use the play to reveal reality in its depths. He plays at unreality in order to cloud the children's minds, to conceal reality, and to encourage them in the unreal. He is misery and confusion, recruiting.[4]

## O Brother, Where Art Thou?

Progressives of a certain kind—of a certain kind, note—were once in the vanguard of realism. Where are they now?

My reading of Christian progressives from the 1880s, up through the end of the First World War, suggests that in matters regarding the family they were doggedly down to earth. Hence their insistence that the Mormons of Utah renounce bigamy, as the price to be paid for the territory's admission to the union of states. Hence their rapprochement to Catholic social teaching as promoted by Pope Leo XIII, and their suspicion of libertarian ideologies having to do with the wallet or the bed. The Divorce Reform League, founded by the Congregationalist minister Samuel Dike in 1881, came into being because the divorce rate in New England had risen to nearly 5 percent. Think of that for a moment. Dike and his fellows knew that in this most determinative feature of a culture, the leniency or irresponsibility of one state would set an evil precedent for others. It would be like a hole punched in the keel of a ship. It hardly matters

---

[4] The Drag Queen Story Hour's website makes no effort to hide the fact that this program is meant to introduce children to the idea that you can be whatever sex you want. For instance, on the "About" page, it says, "DQSH captures the imagination and play of the gender fluidity of childhood and gives kids glamorous, positive, and unabashedly queer role models. In spaces like this, kids are able to see people who defy rigid gender restrictions and imagine a world where people can present as they wish, where dress up is real." "About," Drag Queen Story Hour, last visited March 26, 2020, https://www.dragqueenstoryhour.org/#about.

where the hole is punched. Nevada and not Maine would set the standard for the nation, and it would be the magnet for people wanting an easy out.

It was during these years also that Anthony Comstock, with broad support from both major parties, waged his largely successful war against pornographic literature and films, and contraceptive devices. So-called Comstock laws were instituted all over the country, and it was one of those laws that a pair of Planned Parenthood operatives challenged in *Griswold v. Connecticut*, decided by the Supreme Court in 1965. From that decision has arisen a juridical and cultural world of unreality. The old progressives understood much that has since been abandoned. They knew that men and women were not the same. They knew that the health of a free people depended far less upon its politicians than upon the health and vitality and far-reaching influence of the family. They knew that changes in labor, brought about in the wake of the Industrial Revolution, had posed an unprecedented threat to the family by removing the father from the home for most of the day, six days a week. They knew that other developments, even when beneficent in intent, such as the Sunday school movement, the compulsory schooling movement, and calls for the welfare of citizens in distress to be secured by national measures, would take from the family, one after another, its immemorial functions and reduce it to a mere emotional arrangement, a shadow of its true self. Hence, Dike and his colleagues kept the women's suffrage movement at arm's length, because they feared that the family would be supplanted altogether by the individual:

> The more strictly political problem of the family is, if anything, still farther from our present views of public questions. Democracies necessarily part with the political

significance of families as Europe understands the idea.
Among us has culminated that prolonged social movement
by which the family has surrendered its early political functions to build the city, the State, and the nation. And we
are now confronting the question whether the last point
shall not be yielded, and by the enfranchisement of women
secure the completed substitution of the individual for the
family as the ultimate and only true depositary of the pre-
rogatives of political power.[5]

They might be accused of excessive caution. In the event,
it seems that those more cautious among them were pre-
scient. They turned always to what they argued was plain
reality; they did not propose a new order of the sexes.

The law challenged in *Griswold* had long lain unenforced.
That does not mean it was idle. It expressed the people's
opinion on contraception, and no doubt it depressed the
sale of the pharmacopoeia of contraceptive pills and poi-
sons and balloons. Nevertheless, the Supreme Court ruled
that the state could not intrude itself upon the sacrosanct
realm of the marriage bed. Justice Douglas sounded like a
church divine, or an old lady in lace, when he wrote, "Would
we allow the police to search the sacred precincts of marital
bedrooms for telltale signs of the use of contraceptives? The
very idea is repulsive to the notions of privacy surrounding
the marriage relationship." True it is—it was the state's interest in *upholding the sanctity of marriage* that Justice Douglas
put forward as the grounds for legalizing contraception.

That was the first step into unreality. It was taken alongside a step into the constitutionally unreal. Douglas knew
that there was no language in the Constitution that bore
upon sexual matters one way or the other. So he divined the

[5] "Problems of the Family", *Century Magazine*, January 1890.

right to pharmaceutical and mechanical contraception from shadows of shadows, his magical mystical "penumbras", emanating from the document. I am trying to imagine what penumbras might similarly be found to emanate from a labor contract or from testimony under oath, penumbras that would permit their discoverers to do as they pleased. This divination was not law or legal reasoning but the sleight of hand of a mountebank, the quick chatter of a charlatan. It was also a violation of the people's right to govern themselves. We have legislators, and many of them too, in villages, boroughs, towns, cities, counties, and states, and to them we refer all pragmatic questions, not to the judiciary. For there is no reason to suppose that experience in the minutiae of the law makes you an expert in marriage. I would not have asked Justice Douglas to wire my house. Yet our current polity, with weak legislatures, dug-in and unaccountable bureaucracies, and judges led by their nose for the social airs of the time, is like a house whose walls and floors have been fitted out by a few theorists who could not tell oak from pine or granite from chalk. "That won't work", or "That will cause more harm than good", are not objections that the judges recognize. They give forth their ideas and then retire to their mansions, rulers as they are. *Fiat judicium, ruat caelum.*

Let us return to the marital unreality that Douglas' decision involves. For there is no reason why marriage should even exist as an institution, were it not for the fact that marriage is *fruitful*. Mother and father make children. They do the child-making thing. That is what sexual intercourse is. Marriage has no biological purpose otherwise. I will go so far as to say that even fruitless marriages have social significance in their modeling the fruitful. That the child-making thing is enjoyable, and that it helps to bind man and woman together, is all to the good, but sexual intercourse remains what it is regardless of the enjoyment. Douglas was purporting to defend marriage by undermining the very reason why man has instituted marriage to begin with. The old progressives would have seen the error and called him on it, but this was 1965, and the state of Connecticut itself put up only a halfhearted defense of the old law.

Now it is at least a form of legal reasoning to argue that there are all kinds of protections of marriage built into the common law, including even the assumption that marriage is holy. A wife may not, for instance, be required to testify against her husband. But it is remarkable to observe with what breathless haste the courts then abandoned any touching regard for marriage. In *Roe v. Wade* (1973), they ripped from the husband any say in the matter of his wife's decision to kill their unborn child. Perhaps that is because in each case legal reasoning of a sort was put forward for the nonce, without much concern either for consistency or for that holiness that so overawed the court in *Griswold*.

In saying that the decision in *Griswold* was based on at least some shade of legal reasoning, I do not imply that the decision was sound. For the court assumed what it could not have any grounds or any expertise for assuming—namely, that the holiness of marriage would be safeguarded by making contraceptives available to all. The court was well aware that you could not sell contraceptives only to married people; that would be both discriminatory and unenforceable, and in fact the court said as much in *Eisenstadt v. Baird* (1972). The result was what we see now: people delay marriage longer and longer, enjoying the marital act without having to sacrifice themselves for the marital reality; and inevitably the tricksy devices will fail, or people lulled into a false sense of security fail to use them, and millions of children are born out of wedlock, 40 percent of all children in the United States as of the early twenty-first century.

Surely that could have been predicted even back in those days—and it was predicted, a few years after *Griswold*, by Pope Paul VI, in *Humanae vitae* (1968). Essentially, then, the court decided that marriage was such a holy institution, and the relations between husband and wife were so private, that husbands and wives and everybody else in Connecticut could not preserve what was then a rather modest law designed *to protect the institution of marriage.*

The court could well say that the Connecticut law would not in fact protect marriage; could say it then, perhaps, blocking their ears with wax and binding their eyes with blindfolds. But if that was the court's position, then the court was no longer a court but a board of social work, a town council for the country, a legislative body made of unelected officials with no better insight into the subtleties of the relations between the sexes than that possessed by your next-door neighbor. That too is reality. As I repeat, our judges are supposed to know about law. They can pretend to no special knowledge about any other feature of human existence. It was *Griswold,* and not *Roe v. Wade,* that first ensconced in American jurisprudence the fundamental principles of the sexual revolution.

All Christians, not only renegade and softheaded Catholics, would do well to reconsider whether God would permit a thing whose consequences would be so widespread and so devastating. I speak in charity here; I think the matter requires deep and humble rethinking. No comparisons with Prohibition, please: for a little wine is good for the stomach, and Jesus did not turn the fruit of the vine into water. Alcohol is a perilous good that can be abused. Contraception, a *good* that can be abused? What good? And how great the evil that has come!

## Outrage in Canuckistan

Unreality is hard to contain.

In 2010, Marc Ouellet, cardinal of Quebec, tried, in clear yet characteristically temperate language, to reopen in Canada discussion of abortion. It was heartening to hear any of the Canadian prelates speaking about this or any other moral issue. That is because Canada, my longtime summer home, suffers impediments to discussion that are even worse than those in the United States. If religious people in America think that the television media and the newspapers and the gray old weeklies like *Time* are against them, that is nothing compared with the homogeneous secularism of the media in Canada. Government in Canada keeps strict watch over which people are granted broadcast licenses, and what programs will be aired. The result is that there basically is no such thing as talk radio north of the border—only a few innocuous shows here and there. It took many years for the Catholic network EWTN to win permission from Ottawa to be placed on the docket for cable television. For a while, the bitter jest was that EWTN was broadcast everywhere in the world but Red China and Canada. Religious programming on the major networks is minimal; the ineffectual and oh-so-gingerly feminist *100 Huntley Street* comes to mind. Whatever one may think of the virtues and vices of Fox News, the *Washington Times*, the Heritage Foundation, and Christian radio, in Canada such countervailing voices, whether so-called conservative, genuinely conservative, or religious, are not to be heard.

Canadians also groan under the yoke of their new Charter of Rights, and the presumptuous interpretations of said charter by their supreme court. Someone should hold up for Burkean analysis this ill-conceived and amnesiac document for empowering the central government or, worse, unelected courts, ostensibly to protect individual rights but actually to enshrine a view of the individual as radically independent of culture, the family, the community, and any moral law whatsoever regarding sexuality. As for the Catholic Church in Canada, it long ago made a devil's bargain with the government, accepting federal money while capitulating to increasingly intrusive federal regulations and court decisions. In some parts of Canada—in Nova Scotia, where we live—there are no Catholic schools at all. After Pope Paul VI issued *Humanae vitae*, reaffirming the Church's perennial condemnation of sexual unreality, the Canadian prelates, as did the Americans, met to issue a veto on the pope, in the so-called Winnipeg Statement.

So then, Cardinal Ouellet made his temperate remarks about abortion. The media erupted in outrage. Then ensued something that was disappointing and entirely predictable. Other Church officials straightaway tried to explain what the cardinal meant and did not mean. They fell over themselves to reassure people that they understood the "tragedy" of abortion, and the anguish suffered by women who face an unwanted child. They gave the game away. One fellow even implied that, in conscience, women cannot be held accountable for abortion when abortion is the only choice available.

"Only choice": what can that mean? Let us look at reality.

If you have a cow and you put her in the field with a bull, what do you expect will happen? If you pump the cow's body with estrogens to try to fool her body into a "pregnancy" that does not exist, and the cow's body triumphs over your deception, how is that a failure? Surely the choice is the initial one: whether to do the child-making thing to begin with, or, to continue with my analogy from husbandry, to put the cow in the field.

Let us continue with the reality of human motivations. Canada is a great welfare state. All kinds of support, public and private, are available for unwed mothers. Partly as a result of this generosity, unwed mothers are everywhere. In Cardinal Ouellet's province of Quebec, more than half of all children are born out of wedlock. The rate in the rest of Canada is not too far behind. Allan Carlson, founder of the Howard Center for Family, Religion, and Society, has pointed out that the welfare state initiated in the United States under Franklin Roosevelt was initially quite friendly to marriage and to the father-headed household. It was characterized, he says, by a maternalism of the Left, nor was it peculiar to the United States. He has interesting things to say about socialist women in Sweden, who marched for living wages for their husbands, so that they could remain in the home and take care of their children properly. The point here is that a farsighted social welfare policy need not be such as to disintegrate the very thing we wish to assist, the family.

In any case, where is the "tragedy"? What none of the churchmen mention is that fornication is simply a way of life in Canada. Why is Tiffany pregnant? Because Tiffany has been shacking up with her boyfriend for two years. Why is Ashley pregnant? Because she went home with a boy after a party once too often. This is the stuff not of tragedy but of old-fashioned selfishness, irresponsibility, and lust. It is not as if a Canadian woman is walking one day down Dominion Street, and *ping!*—she finds herself with child. Certain preliminaries are, unless I am much mistaken, still requisite.

Of course the joker here is contraception. People are supposed to be protected from the natural consequences of their actions. And when the pill does not work (and, given enough time, it will fail), then abortion is the backup. Imagine a device in a car that limits speed to thirty miles an hour. I wish to get drunk, and to drive home, and so I do the "responsible" thing, which is to turn on the speed-limiting device. That way, I will not be quite so likely to wrap my car around a tree. Now who would say, if I total my car anyway, that I was involved in something wholly accidental? If I did not want to wreck the car, I should not have been drunk behind the wheel. What none of the prelates wanted to say was yet the most obvious thing of all to say. It was to remind people of reality. "If you did not want a child, why were you having sexual intercourse? Why did you take your clothes off? That was not accidental but deliberate."

What then would be the excuse? "I did it because it felt good." "I did it because I could never keep my boyfriend (or girlfriend) if I didn't." "I did it because everybody does it, and it's no big deal." "I did it because I was in love." And for these lame reasons, we are to excuse the offense against prudence, against the proper use of one's sex, and against charity toward the child, who will grow up without the married mother and father he deserves.

And what is supposed to happen, where is the tragedy, if the child is brought to term? Again, we are talking about a welfare state, and one in which there is absolutely no social stigma remaining for bearing a child out of wedlock. More reality. "I will have to quit school for a while." "I will have to quit my job, and my boyfriend will have to work nights." "I will have to go home and live with my mother, and we don't get along." We are talking about matters, not of life and death, but of preferences and conveniences and delayed or discarded plans. I am not saying that it is easy to take care of a baby, particularly when one is not married, and it is always possible to give the child up for adoption. But to call such things tragic is to stretch the word beyond all usefulness. The prelates should say to their charges, "If you do not wish to bear a child, you should not be doing what makes women pregnant." And, "Fornication violates the moral law." Indeed, according to the *Catechism of the Catholic Church*, it is gravely sinful. Which means, barring invincible ignorance, and other spiritual conditions known only to God, those who die unrepentant of the evil will take their sweating places alongside those sodomite priests we all are so scandalized by. Imagine the outcry if the cardinal had said that.

## How Dare We See?

What happened in Quebec got still worse.

In the well-known and wise fable of Hans Christian Andersen, the little boy, who is too young to be able to pretend that he sees what he does not see, or that he does not see what he sees, suddenly cries out, when all the people round about him are too timid to speak, "But he has no clothes on!" The poor emperor knows it too, and blushes. So the story ends.

These days it might be an empress. Women, C. S. Lewis seemed to believe, were less likely than men to pitch themselves into ideology—hence the sensible Christian girl, in

*The Screwtape Letters* (1942), with whom the "patient" falls in love, and who therefore poses a dire threat to the devil's plots to damn him with evil delusions. But Lewis did not take into sufficient account the mass media and the tendency of the sociable sex to follow along. As usual in human life, a strength misapplied becomes a weakness.

The little boy in the fable was fortunate. His emperor did not have a cadre of enforcers working continually to prevent any such outbreak of reality. He had not been browbeaten in the emperor's schools, lest he say what he saw, or lest he should see at all. In Andersen's telling, the people were merely too vain and proud to admit that they could not see those fine and subtle clothes that everyone else seemed to be able to see. It was a kingdom-wide lie. But it did not require a Royal Department of Mendacity. And the people had not yet persuaded themselves, as Winston Smith could almost do, in the dreadful basement room of Orwell's Ministry of Love, that two fingers were three, or three were two.

We have the enforcers of mendacity now. The press is foremost among them. For without constant pressure from organs of mass society, people will rub their eyes and awake from the bad dream. That cannot be permitted.

So, after Cardinal Ouellet offered his opinion, he was immediately attacked. The fury of a certain Patrick Lagacé in an article in *La Presse* may stand as an example for all.[6] First came the old *argumentum ad horologiam*: after the big hand reaches the twelve, the moral law changes and can never return to what it was—which is as much as to say that there is no such thing as the moral law. It is all mere custom. Why anyone should be exercised over mere custom, I do not know. Lagacé and temporalists of his sort do not notice

[6] Patrick Lagacé, "Le mépris de Kazem Ouellet", *La Presse*, May 17, 2010.

that the record of the last century has been singularly ugly. That record should have put to rest forever the notion that mankind's moral progress is uninterrupted and predictable rather than at best fitful, with an advance here marred by degeneracy there. What the author meant, and what he was not honest enough to say, was simply that they in Quebec wanted to rut like dogs in an alley if so they chose, and to the devil or the dumpster with the children they might conceive. Oh, for the heretics of old, who had real substance to them, with whom it was an honor to fight! Now all we have are spoiled and surly libertines.

Then, like the click of a cheap timepiece, came the assertion that Cardinal Ouellet was just like a certain vicious Iranian imam. The truth is the reverse, as Pope Benedict XVI was careful to point out in his famous speech at Regensburg, much misunderstood by an ill-tempered and ill-educated media elite. What our exhausted postmodernity shares with Islam is just that disjunction between reason and will. We Christians do not believe that it is to "fetter" God if we say that he acts according to reason. That is the Muslim interpretation of it, an interpretation that reduces God to pure will. We believe that the wisdom of God is in fact the coeternal Son of the Father. To say that God works according to reason is like saying that his omnipotence is made manifest in power. But, as soon as a Christian's reason dares to venture beyond quantity and technology, the imams of cultural degeneracy are quick to sentence the reasoner to ridicule, calumny, loss of livelihood, and sometimes prison.

Cardinal Ouellet is, like most prelates in the United States and Canada, a moderately liberal fellow, for better and for worse. He accepts most of the assumptions behind a welfare state; he has made his peace with democracy; he views reason and faith as friendly to one another (as do I, naturally);

he believes that one ought to render unto Caesar what is
Caesar's, a command that would be incomprehensible to the
faithful Muslim, for whom the mosque is the state and the
state is the mosque. But he also believes that Christians have
not only the right but the duty to proclaim the moral law,
not for themselves alone but for the common good, regardless of what the current social climate might be. And this,
the journalist Lagacé could not abide. This is what earned
Ouellet the title of "fundamentalist".

One of the characteristics of unreality is ignorance of
history. The past is a check against every utopian dream.
That is not just because the utopian dreams have ended in
disillusion, as at Brook Farm, or nightmare, as in the Soviet Union. It is because the past is the unalterable record of
man. It shows us what human nature is. The past, in the case
of fundamentalism, is neither distant nor hard to interpret.
In the early twentieth century, reacting against a dilution of
Christian teaching that would reduce the Trinity to an uneasy unity, the gospel to a call for moral and social change,
the crucifixion to a terrible governmental error, and the person of Christ to a great teacher, Protestant scholars such as
J. Gresham Machen reaffirmed classic Christian teachings,
the "fundamentals". Machen believed, as did several Catholic popes before him, that liberalism, in part sprung from
Christianity, was now a solvent for it. Earnest Christians
on the other side accused the fundamentalists of pessimism.
But if we are to judge by the consequences, the so-called
pessimists were correct. All the liberal denominations are
moribund. To call for the Catholic Church to abandon the
fundamentals *after* you have seen the practical results elsewhere is essentially to call for her demise. Rather rude, when
you think of it—to condemn a Catholic cardinal for refrain-
ing to take a suicide pill.

Lagacé was not, of course, exercised about the question of the substitutionary atonement of Christ on behalf of man, or the coeternal begetting of the Son from the Father. A "fundamentalist" now is merely somebody who has failed to join the crowd cheering the naked and tumescent emperor. He retains a moral vision that was once common to both liberal and conservative. He simply believes that people do not have the moral right to fornicate or commit adultery. Nor does he believe it is permissible to dispense with the unwanted child that might result. It does not matter that Cardinal Ouellet is not a biblical literalist. It does not matter whether he is a Thomist, after the Laval school of Charles De Koninck, or a Platonizing Christian, after the manner of Dietrich von Hildebrand. It does not matter whether he holds a sunny view of democracy and the Church's relationship to it, as did Jacques Maritain, or whether, like such conservatives as Frederick Wilhelmsen, he views democracy as beset with its own intractable problems. In the world of Western journalism, one does not have to learn anything about the figures one accuses. The Ministry of Truth is too busy saving the world and has no time to learn. Does the cardinal believe that public nudity ought to be outlawed? Fundamentalist! That people should not kill their children in the womb? Fundamentalist! That divorce is a social evil? Fundamentalist!

Who was the fundamentalist here, or rather the bigot, in the old sense of the word, the man so obstreperous and obtuse that he cannot begin to entertain another opinion? Who was performing the equivalent of employing a proof text? Who was divorcing moral assertion from reasoned argument? It is typical of the secular Left, and predictable. When one believes that good and evil are not objective realities to be discovered by the practical reason and to be honored in custom and law, and when, moreover, one dispenses with God's revelation, which does not override reason but clarifies matters for us, giving our reason a boost, then nothing remains but to believe that "good" and "evil" are subjective and relative to the evaluator and his society. I do not mean to say that Lagacé had thought the matter out so explicitly. Thought requires calm, and calm does not sell newspapers. But, absent a law and a Lawgiver to which and to whom we must all, individually and as a people, give homage, the state comes to fill the void, and what is "right" will be determined by those who shout the loudest, or who have the most money, or who fill the positions of greatest prominence and prestige. Moral argument collapses, and people shout, "It's right because I say so!" It is the suasion of the gun.

Had Lagacé stopped there, it would have been bad enough, but he continued, noting that Cardinal Ouellet had also weighed in on end-of-life issues. The cardinal, it seems, does not believe that the state has the right to allow people to kill themselves when they are terribly sick, or, more accurately, to enlist the assistance of physicians in killing themselves.

We are dealing here with a question of ultimate reality. Cardinal Ouellet upheld the inestimable value of every human life, from conception to natural death. Every being of human origin is to be regarded as holy, because every such being *is in fact holy*. We are making a case as to fact. It is those who champion assisted suicide who believe that certain lives are worthless, that their suffering has no value. In *Healing the Culture* (2000), Robert Spitzer, S.J., says that sometimes it is only through suffering that we confess that we are vulnerable and that our hearts go out toward our fellow sufferers in love. The cardinal would understand; the politician raving in the streets would not.

Lagacé ended his article by wishing that Cardinal Ouellet would die "a slow, painful death",[7] so that he would know what it was like to have only skin on your bones and to be vomiting up your own excrement. A slow and painful death . . . like that of Jesus, perhaps? Or that of John Paul II? Or Thérèse of Lisieux? What made the journalist believe that Catholic priests are not frequently in the company of people who are dying, slowly, sometimes with great suffering? The purpose of suffering, said Saint Pope John Paul, was "to unleash love".[8] That the press would print such a vicious wish shows how deeply the realist Christian is hated. Madmen hate those who see through their madness. Unreality is frail. It *must* be backed up with force.

## Babies and Bottle Caps

Those of us who have opposed the snuffing out of young human beings, euphemistically called "abortion" (the word once meant "miscarriage", so that the adjective "induced" had to be added to denote the deliberate act), know quite well that all of biological science is on our side. Dr. Horatio Storer, the father of gynecology in the United States and a convert to the Catholic faith, demonstrated without doubt that the fertilized ovum is its own self-acting organism, that it is alive and not merely potentially alive, that it possesses in latency or in the seed all the powers of the fully grown human being, and that although it is dependent upon the mother for protection and nourishment, it is independent in its being, as shown by its unattached and living passage through the fallopian tube. As soon as that was known, the

---

[7] "Une longue et pénible maladie".

[8] John Paul II, apostolic letter *Salvifici doloris* (February 11, 1984), no. 29.

American Medical Association, at Storer's urging, moved in 1859 to petition the lawmakers of every state in the union to criminalize the act of induced abortion as objectively tantamount to murder. Dr. Storer was a Quaker when he led that crusade. His conversion to the Catholic faith came later.

The unborn child, at whatever stage we wish to name, is not a part of the mother, like a thumb. It has its own genetic code. It does not communicate with the other organs in the mother's body. It is not inert, like an acorn that has not germinated. It is not inanimate, like a stone. It is not a parasite, like a tapeworm—just as puppies in the womb of a bitch are not parasites but the natural and healthy results of the dog's reproduction. It is not a foreign invader of the same species, like Judith Jarvis Thomson's absurd violinist who connects his systems to those of an innocent stranger; again, it is the natural and healthy result of reproduction. It is not dead, like a corpse. It is not equine, like a foal, or ovine, like a lamb, or serpentine, like a politician. It is human. It is a being.

Apologists for abortion, when I was young, used to wag their fingers and say that of course they knew how "tragic" the needful snuffing was. They no longer do so. Now they celebrate it. Liberal church divines used to wring their hands and yield to the supposed tragedy. Now they treat it as sacrament. Feminists stage rallies to boast about the bloodshed. The words of Alexander Pope come to mind:

> Vice is a monster of so frightful mien
> As to be hated needs but to be seen;
> Yet seen too oft, familiar with her face,
> We first endure, then pity, then embrace.[9]

[9] Alexander Pope, "An Essay on Man", epistle 2, lines 217–20.

Therefore, the reality of the evil needs to be placed before our eyes in its full horror.

Sometimes a child is fortunate enough to survive an abortion. One such child, Gianna Jessen, has grown up and will speak to all listeners about how thankful she is that someone saved her. People who toil in the pro-life trenches have heard plenty of stories of nurses instructed to set a surviving baby alone on a tray to gasp out its little life, or to wrap it up and toss it in the refuse. The barbarity of such deeds has sometimes sufficed to jolt those complicit in abortion out of their moral fog, even as it has pitched others deeper into the evil. That is typical of man's response to even the greatest gifts of grace. It is as if the good Lord had reached down through the sanitized dungeons of man's cramped heart to spring upon sinners the surprise of life; and a few people turn toward that gift with grateful hearts. Others reject it; but the rejection in the case of the surviving baby must involve a strenuous effort to shut God out. Says the Father in Milton's *Paradise Lost*, foretelling the action of his grace and some men's refusal to accept it:

> This my long sufferance and my day of grace
> They who neglect and scorn, shall never taste,
> But hard be hardened, blind be blinded more,
> That they may stumble on, and deeper fall;
> And none but such from mercy I exclude.[10]

Hence we now have laws, in New York and Virginia, that protect the mother's intention to kill her child *even if it should have survived the attempt to kill it.* The child will have been born. It poses not even the most imaginary threat to her life or health, no more than if it were on the other side

[10] John Milton, *Paradise Lost*, bk. 3, lines 198–202.

of an ocean. It is breathing, perhaps barely. It is suffering, for certain. It is, by law, a citizen of the United States, granted all the rights that the Constitution and the laws supposedly guarantee. But it shall be left to die. And nice people celebrate its demise.

I believe that our erstwhile president, Mr. Obama, was and is a nice man. It seems that our current president, Mr. Trump, is not a nice man. Niceness, of course, is of no moral value whatsoever. When Mr. Obama was a senator, he regularly voted against laws requiring that doctors and nurses do what is reasonable to save the life of an abortion survivor, or even, as legal scholar Robert George put it, to wrap it in a towel, so that it would be warm as it died. Love is not cold, like a refrigerator for embryos, said Jérôme Lejeune, the brilliant doctor who discovered the cause of Down syndrome and who then became the world's leading advocate for the lives of unborn children with the disorder. Niceness can be downright glacial, with a smile.

Evil is degenerative. It is not and can never be stable, because it is not a presence but an absence. We move from snuffing to manufacture in order to cannibalize. Mr. Obama threw the field open for cloning for experimentation, stipulating that all such human life be destroyed. It was the first time in our history that we enacted a directive not merely allowing but requiring the taking of innocent life.

It also marked another first. This one should not have been hard to see. It is certainly not hard to see now, when homosexual couples have embraced child-manufacture or child-stock-breeding with defiant insouciance. Perhaps C. S. Lewis' *Abolition of Man* ought to be on every Christian's reading list, once a year. The very act of cloning or genetic manipulation reduces human beings to instruments for our utility, or to products of manufacture, like bottle caps. We

C.S. Lewis

cannot transcend our nature by our own will without, in the supposed act of transcendence itself, sinking below humanity—and in the case of the industrialization of human life, sinking below the animals in the wild, to the status of a cheese on the shelf of a grocery store. I am not warning about the Brave New World to come, when scientists will do as they please so long as there is money in it, a world wherein everyone is "free" from the commandments of God and the dictates of the natural law and is therefore enslaved to the unrestrained power of evil or stupid men, or of the mechanisms they fashion and that they cannot control. That world is here already. Witness merry old England, allowing scientists to create human-animal hybrids—and not the asses that have always sat in the world's parliaments, either. A statesman of some vision might see it and ask the simple question, "Why?"

Who has that vision? Only someone committed to reality can have it. But the sexual revolution is in the cause of unreality, of the grim fantasies of hedonism, followed by disillusionment, apathy, and, except for the grace of God, embittered and lonely old men and women, whose bodies may not engage in the acts anymore but whose hearts are not one degree purer for their enforced abstinence. Says Shakespeare:

> Th' expense of spirit in a waste of shame
> Is lust in action; and till action, lust
> Is perjured, murderous, bloody, full of blame,
> Savage, extreme, rude, cruel, not to trust,
> Enjoyed no sooner but despisèd straight,
> Past reason hunted; and, no sooner had,
> Past reason hated as a swallowed bait
> On purpose laid to make the taker mad;

Mad in pursuit and in possession so,
Had, having, and in quest to have, extreme;
A bliss in proof and proved, a very woe;
Before, a joy proposed; behind, a dream.
 All this the world well knows; yet none knows well
 To shun the heaven that leads men to this hell.[11]

But when Obama was asked what he would do if one of his daughters were to become pregnant before she was married, he did not turn to the bracing lessons of the past. He replied instead that he would be disappointed but that he would not want to "punish her with a child". I am sure that half my countrymen would agree. I fear that nearly half those who call themselves Catholics would agree. But that phrase reveals a lot: "punish her with a child". I wish someone would punish me with a grandchild. Can you be punished with a Rembrandt? But a child is far more beautiful than is anything that any artist has ever accomplished. That is no exaggeration but the flat truth.

Obama showed no sense of a duty broken. He seemed not to be aware of duty at all. He was not revolutionary in this regard—just like the general run of unthinking and selfish and apathetic Americans. He seemed not to recognize the duty not to pretend to be married when one is not married; a duty we owe to one another and to our Maker. He showed no sense of a sin that requires conversion of heart. No sense of the holiness of sex, and the holiness of the child conceived. No sense that that child, if loved aright (and that love might well require giving it to a mother and a father who could care for it better), could be a lifeline thrown to the wretched sinner by the Lord God. No sense that that child comes as it were from another world, to break

[11] William Shakespeare, Sonnet 129.

through that hardest of objects in creation, the human heart. None of that; man is valued for utility instead. The child either is or is not instrumental to the fulfillment of my appetites. If it is not, it may be disposed of. Preferably not on a stainless steel tray, gulping for air, but if that's what it takes, then that's what it takes. No one should be punished with the disappointment of appetite. "Suffer the little children to come unto me", says Jesus (Mk 10:14). "Except ye be converted, and become as little children, ye shall not enter into the kingdom of heaven" (Mt 18:3). Mary bore her firstborn child and laid him in a manger. "I wouldn't want to punish her with a child", says Obama. Half the nation agrees. Think of it, young person who may be reading these words.

## We'll Just Relieve You of Those, Sir

In these times of sexual unreality, where are the churches? Where they have so often been, floating along. Or taking the world's lead, or pandering to its desires. The Church stands best for the world when, like the good Earl of Kent, she braves it, and tells it to its face that it does evil. So Kent says to the old King Lear, who believed the flattery of his elder daughters and rejected the truth-telling of the daughter who truly loved him:

> Thy youngest daughter does not love thee least,
> Nor are those empty-hearted whose low sounds
> Reverb no hollowness.[12]

---

[12] William Shakespeare, *King Lear*, Ignatius Critical Editions (San Francisco: Ignatius Press, 2008), act 1, scene 1, lines 154–56.

But that is no pleasant task. Kent is banished for his pains
—for his love. He is not like the timeserver Oswald, whom
he would beat for his brazen cowardice:

> Such smiling rogues as these,
> Like rats, oft bite the holy cords atwain
> Which are too intrince to unloose; smooth every passion
> That in the natures of their lords rebel,
> Bring oil to fire, snow to the colder moods;
> Renege, affirm, and turn their halcyon beaks
> With every gale and vary of their masters,
> Knowing naught, like dogs, but following.[13]

The churches have been far more like Oswald than like
Kent. They have been weather vanes to the wind, and not
like brave captains to use that wind itself to make headway
against it. The world has raised the hoop, and the poodle
jumps.

Let me give an example. Some years ago, the wise heads
of the Christians for Biblical Equality declared that eunuchs
have something to teach the Church. Indeed.

The Church, that old gal in lavender print, has labored
under the quaint misconstruction that God created man in
the beginning, and male and female he created them. Not so,
said the gelders and spayers at Christians for Biblical Equality. There is an intermediate class of people, once known as
hermaphrodites or androgynes, possessing the sexual characteristics of both sexes. So it was as the Catholic author
David Mills commented: a birth defect is elevated to the status of the normal, just so that we can tear down the whole
idea of the normal. We must concentrate on the outlandish,

[13] Ibid., 2.2.75–82.

so that we can ignore or traduce the normal and consign reality to oblivion.

The point was not to ensure that men and women would be regarded as equal, supposing that equality of all persons in the grace of God is to be held by faith. I mostly doubt it. I am not the equal of Mary, or of any woman saint I might name. But I think that the Christians for Biblical Equality were not about equality. They were about unreality.

For the very word "equal" implies distinction. If two things are identical, we do not say they are equal, unless we are dealing with mathematical objects and speaking somewhat informally. Back in high school we were taught trigonometric "identities"—for instance, that the square of the tangent was the same as the square of the secant, minus one. We say "equal", but what we really mean is "identical": they are in fact *the same thing*. But when we are not talking about identities, an assertion of equality is an assertion either of some measurable quantity or of some metaphysical characteristic. So what must the equalitarians be talking about?

Not some measurable quantity. It is abundantly clear that males and females are not the same. It is what a member of an alien race would notice first about us. It is the first thing we notice about someone we meet, and the last thing we forget. So constitutive of our being human is our sex! Men and women are not, as groups, quantitatively or qualitatively the same in height, muscle mass, vocal pitch, hairiness, bone density, and adrenal performance; age and pattern of maturation to puberty are also different. Their wrists are different, their larynxes, their teeth, their skin, their hair, their reproductive organs—as someone ought to point out, perhaps with helpful diagrams, to people of our time who are confused. But that might not work, either—as we are now to believe that a man can possess a womb too.

Men and women use different areas of the brain to do things as simple as to come up with rhymes, remember names, or total up a list of numbers. They laugh differently, and at many different things. One could spend all one's life studying and appreciating these delightful differences. Indeed, plenty of poets and artists have done just that.

So it must be a metaphysical characteristic, then, that makes men and women equal in any meaningful sense. What might that be? Well, all Christians have affirmed that men and women have been created in the image and likeness of God, and while some medieval thinkers suggested that perhaps the man was a *closer* image of God than the woman, that idea is about unheard of now. (Unless I am mistaken, it was never popular in the East—for instance, in Gregory of Nyssa.) Rather, Pope Saint John Paul II suggested that man would not, alone, have constituted a being made in God's image and likeness; in the complementarity and union of male and female, mankind mirrors the Trinity. Be that as it may, there is no controversy whatever, on this score, between the equalitarians and faithful Catholics or Orthodox or Protestants who take seriously the distinctions between men and women as they apply to order in the family and the Church.

What is left, then, is not so much an assertion of equality as an assertion of indifference. Let's say I have two cars, one red, one blue. They are not the same car. They are not "equal" in a quantitative sense—not even if they are the same make and model. But, for the purposes for which I require the car—I want to drive to the local pizza place and pick up a couple of pies for supper—the cars should be construed as equal. That is, it makes no difference whether the cars are red and blue, or Ford and Chrysler, or Fiat and Porsche.

We are to believe, then, that all those things that make men recognizably male, and women recognizably female, are matters of indifference. For some practical purposes, no doubt some of them are. If you want to twirl an uncooked pizza crust, it will hardly matter if you have a baritone voice (though it might help to have big hands, and a knack for juggling would not hurt, either). If you have to lull a baby to sleep, it will hardly matter if your hair is glossy and fine (though it might help to have a gentle voice, and an instinct carefully attuned to the needs of small things like babies). But the pavers at Christians for Biblical Equality were not thinking about those unimportant things. They were probably not even thinking about toting a rifle and ammunition or hauling an unconscious adult out of a burning building and down a ladder. They were thinking about such prestigious things as being presidents and priests and generals and chiefs, belonging to the executive branch of the race. If you assert loudly enough that sex is a matter of indifference in a priest or minister, then the congregation will themselves treat it with indifference. I agree—the congregation do eventually treat it with indifference. But then they indifferently walk away—or people never show up to begin with. David Blankenhorn, the liberal Democrat who, before he capitulated on the matter of homosexual unions, once championed the cause of fatherhood in America, discovered this very indifference among some men he interviewed. They most positively insisted that a woman could be a perfectly fine head of a household, no question about it. These same men were also most positively in prison when they said it.

What most intrigues me about the consequences of egal-

itarianism, though, is that even indifference will not suffice. We are not allowed to say that maleness and femaleness do not matter. After all, so long as we say *that*, we are
continuing to notice maleness and femaleness, and we might
come under their spell. We might conclude that wonder and
reverence and reveling in our inequalities (and this works
both ways) are a great deal more fun and a great deal more,
well, *realistic* than indifference. Hence, we must efface the
very notions of maleness and femaleness. We must do the
same thing that homosexual activists used to do with sexual propensities: we place them on a sliding scale, so that
nobody is really anything in particular.

At which point I fail to see why we should retain any categories of being at all. A. J. Freddoso, in his excellent introduction to the Renaissance philosopher Francisco Suárez,
returns again and again to the contradictions inherent in
contemporary empiricism, its "epistemic despair", and its
lapsing into absurd violations of common sense. For just
as the egalitarian trowel-wielders want dearly to reduce talk
of men and women to matters of amendable convention,
so the contemporary empiricists have no sensible way to
talk about what in everyday parlance are called recognizable
"things", without reducing them to aggregates of inherently
meaningless matter. So we return to the point I made at the
beginning of this chapter. If we cannot talk about men and
women, why should we hold our incapacity at that line?
What sense can it make to talk about human beings at all,
especially when technopolitan hybrids are looming on the
horizon? Why not have a sliding scale there too?

That, I am sure, was not in the field of vision of the
people at Christians for Biblical Equality, and their champi-
onship of the androgyne—why not, I do not really know,
other than that they were shortsighted and not given to

consider the implications of the latest fashions. Scientistic atheists these days have come to admit that even though there are no such things in actuality as definably human beings, we should act as if there were; even though the notion of a free will is incomprehensible to materialists, we should suppose in our laws and customs that there is such a thing; even though there is no such thing as a "thing", properly speaking, it would make life impossible for us if we abandoned that common sense position; we should even, according to a review of the atheist Alain de Botton in *First Things*, have cathedrals and holy days and feasts dedicated to secular heroes, even though religion itself makes no sense.[14] We are to live in a meaningless world as if there were meaning. The sexual egalitarians take the argument in quite the opposite direction. We are, in the instance of man and woman, to live in a meaningful world as if it were meaningless.

[14] Alan Jacobs, "A Religion for Atheists," *First Things*, February 2009, https://www.firstthings.com/article/2009/02/002-a-religion-for-atheists.

# 3

# Unreality for Sale

All of our knowledge, said Thomas Aquinas, comes to us first through the senses. He did not mean that the senses were always to be trusted. All of your knowledge of the world outside your home, if you are a three-year-old child, might come to you from your mother and father, and your mother and father might tell you that the earth sits upon a stack of turtles and that there is a man in the moon, who lives there with his dog and his bush.

The old materialist Lucretius, like his master Epicurus, was somewhat embarrassed by the fact that our senses can be deceived. After all, if the world is made up of matter alone, then the prime sense is not vision, that most ethereal and intellectual of the five, but touch: the sense you get when foot strikes rock. So the Epicureans were good at imagining, for example, how a lump of iron might be made up of atoms with a lot of hooks to catch each other and clinch, or how water might be made up of roly-poly atoms that spill about like a mound of poppy seeds. Their guesses in that regard were sometimes inspired, and in fact the reason why we have water droplets (and therefore streams, rivers, ponds, lakes, and oceans) is that the water molecule, that wondrous thing, is just a little bent by the two hydrogen atoms veering away from each other's slightly positive charge, each having lent, so to speak, its sole negative charge, its electron, to the molecule as a whole. So water is slightly sticky, with just enough surface tension to bead up.

But when it came to imagining the size of the sun, the Epicureans, not well versed in mathematics or astronomy, gave up. If they could not touch it, they were not interested in it. Lucretius says, vaguely and with no real interest, that the sun is, well, just about as big as it appears to our eyes to be, maybe a little bigger or a little smaller. It is no wonder that Cicero looked upon the Epicureans with what went from vague bemusement to curt dismissal. The intellectual life is too important to be given over to appearances.

That most people judge by appearances, we all know well. We *must* judge by appearances. If we had to wait for material or logical demonstration, we would never undertake a single action. The dog sees the shape of a person passing by on the other side of the window. It is the meter reader. The dog barks as if it were a thief. Justly so.

The problem in our time is not that we are taken in by shows. King Lear in his madness saw that trouble:

> Through tattered clothes small vices do appear;
> Robes and furred gowns hide all. Plate sin with gold,
> And the strong lance of justice hurtless breaks.
> Arm it in rags, a pigmy's straw does pierce it.[1]

And what evil is there that has not robed itself in light? Such shows not only fool people into accepting evil; they make them wary of accepting the good. So says the noble young Malcolm in *Macbeth*, when he seeks to determine whether Macduff can be trusted:

> Angels are bright still, though the brightest fell;
> Though all things foul would wear the brows of grace,
> Yet grace must still look so.[2]

---

[1] Shakespeare, *King Lear*, 4.6.166–69.

[2] William Shakespeare, *Macbeth*, ed. Barbara A. Mowat and Paul Werstine (New York: Simon and Schuster, 2013), act 4, scene 3, lines 27–29.

Glass casts diamond into doubt; the glitter slanders the gold. Some people cannot bear to see a man on his knees, praying, because there have been hypocrites. So they play-act at being too wise to fall for the show and end up being hypocrites to the second power. Says the poet Burns, spying a louse crawling to the tip-top of a lady's bonnet in church:

> O wad some Power the giftie gie us
> To see oursels as others see us!
> It wad frae monie a blunder free us
> An' foolish notion:
> What airs in dress an' gait wad lea'e us,
> And ev'n Devotion![3]

A picture says a thousand words, and nine hundred ninety-nine of them may be false. None of this is news. What is different now?

What Richard Weaver called the Great Stereopticon is what is different. A stereopticon is an old device for viewing special two-framed cards stereoptically, that is, as if it were in three dimensions in front of you, so you could pretend to have the experience of looking at goatherds along the Indus River, from your living room, as if you were right there. Calvin called the human heart a factory of idols, those flimsy things that we gaze upon and worship, entirely unreal. Mass media, the Great Stereopticon, is by comparison a vast and astonishingly productive industry of idols, of flashes upon the screen, so easy to look upon, so mesmerizing in their effect, that by contrast the woodcut designs that decorated old books were as a drop in the comprehensive ocean of visual flagella that now whip and sting us and will not let us be. Until our time, an idol was a phantasm, an untruth. "Eyes have they, but they see not: they have ears, but they hear not", says the psalmist, adding, "They that make them

[3] Robert Burns, "To a Louse", lines 43–48.

are like unto them; so is every one that trusteth in them"
(Ps 115:5–6, 8). Now everyone strives to be an idol: *American Idol* was the name of the show on which modestly talented young people would whine and writhe, as if that were to sing like Caruso. They longed to be judged worthy of continuing to compete, with much flash and glare. I doubt that anybody on that show ever sat down soberly to play Beethoven on a piano. At least Schroeder of happy memory had a German idol with eyes and ears and an immense capacity for beauty.

## Singing in the Rainy Graveyard

I am not as pessimistic as Weaver was when it comes to the potentiality of film, his principal villain in the Stereopticon, to make great art. I note, though, that drama is a shy bird. After its glorious invention in the Athens of Aeschylus, Sophocles, and Euripides, and its echo in the Hellenistic Rome of Plautus and Terence, the drama retired for many centuries, only to be born again in a popular movement that spread across Europe when Pope Honorius declared the new triduum of the feast of Corpus Christi. Drama appears to need something like that to thrive. We cannot understand its blossoming forth in ancient Athens apart from the popular energies of self-government, the turn of philosophy toward ultimate questions of human life, and the still-vital traditions of a religious people. We cannot understand its resurgence in the Renaissance apart from those centuries of popular tradition that followed upon the decree of Honorius, or apart from the rediscovery of many classical texts that had been forgotten or lost, or apart from the energies of a post-Reformation world struggling with essential matters of the Christian faith.

Similarly, I think that we cannot understand the so-called Golden Age of Hollywood, which I place between 1935 and 1965, apart from several important good things that Hollywood did not produce. A popular drama was in place already; every small city had its stage, and when the Italians came to America, they brought their opera houses with them. My copies of the *Century Magazine* include serialized autobiographies of the famous comic actor John Joseph Jefferson and the Italian tragedian Tommaso Salvini. Consider: No magazine could hope to keep its subscribers if they were not going to be interested in long-running series describing the lives of such men. But the subscribers were interested. After all, the acting companies *took the show on the road*, crossing the nation and putting on performances in Louisville and Peoria and Wichita. When Thomas Edison invented his "talking machine", the editors of the *Century* looked forward to the time, soon to come, when people need not travel to Bayreuth or Vienna to hear the music of Wagner made real by the most notable conductors of the time but could hear it in their homes *and compare the realizations* for their acuity and taste.

Then there was the energy of the American people, and their still-strong social institutions mediating between the dissociated individual and the state. It is hard to live in a drama when you hardly live in a social world at all. When Mr. Smith went to Washington in the film of that name, he went as a representative who had lived among real people who came together regularly to get real things done, and only such a people could have mobilized hundreds of Scouts to print broadsheets of support and to circulate them across the state of South Dakota. When Sergeant Alvin York was recruited by the Army to fight in World War I, he served for the country he loved, not for an ideology, and when he with his eagle eye had distinguished himself in seizing a nest of German machine gunners, single-handed, he took in stride the accolades he won and returned to his home in Tennessee to farm. You could make a story out of York's youthful drinking and brawling, his conversion to a deep Christian faith, his glory on the battlefield, and his return to a simple life, because it was all rooted in real things, among people whom he knew.

And finally, religious faith. Atheists accuse believers of taking leave of the world around them. The charge is baseless. Where you find saints, you find people steeped in reality. The saints plunge too deeply into the world for our comfort. Saint André Bessette was one such saint. He left his home in Quebec at age eighteen to find work in textile mills in New England, ending up, among the various towns where he lived, in the village of Phenix, Rhode Island, working at its enormous mill during the day, and during the evening prostrating himself in prayer. That mill was burned to the ground by an arsonist in 2005; I culled some bricks from the wreckage to line our front sidewalk, and some stones to build a retaining wall for a garden. I believe that Brother André would have approved. He was a very small man and never in good health, so that he had a hard time persuading the superiors at the Congregation of Holy Cross in Montreal to admit him as a brother. They gave in at last, thinking that if he could not do hard work, at least he could do hard prayer. He did both. It is said that André Bessette cured over ten thousand people by anointing them with oil sanctified to Saint Joseph, in a life crowded with persons and their stories. He died at the age of ninety-one, just before the advent of television. The point is that even the actors who worked in Hollywood had memories, if not the regular experience, of bending their knees in prayer beside their neighbors and being at least fitfully aware of such people as Saint André Bessette. This was while atheist delusions in the Soviet Union had already drenched the earth in blood.

Those conditions no longer apply. The Great Stereopticon not only is detached from reality; it produces an alternate reality, or an unreality, an offense to reality. Only in such an age would certain forms of madness ever get any purchase on men's minds. It is no longer that the screen makes real lives visible to us, or that a Bishop Sheen could be the best-loved personality on television for his amiable and eloquent sermons. It is rather that the screen dictates to us what we see and what we do not see, what we take for real and what we shall overlook entirely. It is the un-teacher to the world: base, shallow, fretful, blaring, instigating, jogging, lurid, mendacious, fantastic but not imaginative, self-serious but not self-examining, a conscience without consciousness, a judge without reason, an idol without beauty, all-invasive yet settled in no sure place, all-affirming yet profoundly ignorant, the foundation of a culture that is no culture, insistently present to us but without a past, grasshoppers that have eaten all the corn.

## For Wales?

I confess that the unreal screen has its gravitational pull and that sometimes I am like a shred of cosmic shrapnel, about to be absorbed by the gaseous giant called Jupiter. We are all this way, we who gaze into the Stereopticon. What is that like? Let me describe an instance.

Once, in 2011, I watched the Super Bowl with the sound off. It was nice not having my nerves jangled by computer-generated whooshes and bombastic apocalyptic football music and the vocal alarms of the announcer as the teams moved from crisis to crisis, turning point to turning point, and so forth. I like football, not the sale of football. Call it a weakness.

I heard later that the pop star who was supposed to sing the national anthem at the beginning of the game blew it. I will bet, though there was no way to confirm this, that she did not understand what the words meant. She would hardly be alone. Probably not one citizen in fifty can tell to what battle the song is a memorial, and in what war. But Old Glory sells, and if I had to choose the least offensive of our sales pitches, the national anthem might be it.

I did also glance at the commercials. Richard Dawkins has said that our bodies are just the machines our genes have built so that they might survive. That is foolish. But perhaps he was thinking about television and commercials. Edward R. Murrow once lamented that television was a medium with great potential, but the reality was little more than a wasteland. He said so at a time when the networks had filled their lineups with attempts to revive the old playhouse and bring it into the living room (or, increasingly, the gazing room): *Playhouse 90*, *The Ford Theater*, *Texaco Playhouse*, and so on. The fear was that television shows were merely vehicles whereby the commercial parasite could be introduced into your volitional system, bypassing the intellect, not to mention ordinary sociability and an encounter with real things. The commercial is the dog, and the program the tail.

Hucksters reveal what they think about their patsies by the methods they use to sell them things. If the patsy considers himself a rational agent, the huckster gives him a spritz of numbers to daze his eyes withal. If the patsy is led by his passions, the huckster gives him a patch of naked flesh to gaze upon. If the patsy is a zealot, the huckster gives him someone convenient to hate. So what did the hucksters of the football game identify as the prime movers of their patsies? The halftime show gave that one away. I asked myself, "If I were a creature from another planet, or, more outlandish still, somebody transported to this day from 1940, what would I guess about the people who apparently find this stuff appealing?" Let's see, then. If such things are evidence, I'd say, "Their favorite color is black— they film everything as if under a metallic blackness. They enjoy spitefulness and cruelty. They don't really understand human creativity. They confuse it with bells and whistles and cheap tricks. They put no premium on kindness, grace, gentleness, nobility. Their women are harsh, while their men are either softheaded boors or monsters. There is nothing childlike in them. They think they appreciate the beauty of the human form, but that is not so. They wish to transform it into something mechanical. They will say that they are just joking with all this business, but that too is revealing. Why should they find nastiness and spitefulness funny?"

It occurs to me that the halftime show sells to Americans what Americans envision themselves to be. It is a frightful thought. Almost fifty years ago I watched one of our local high school bands perform for the halftime of a nationally televised football game. The band was neither ugly nor expensive. No doubt its members did not have the same technical talent as was on display for the Super Bowl. But then, the people liked them, perhaps because they too reflected what the people thought they themselves were, at their best or sweetest. Americans thought they were decent, more or less wholesome, fairly innocent people who appreciated a good job but who did not take either the game or the entertainment as if it were to provide some kind of religious experience. They had gone to their church services in the morning to get that. Some of them did, anyway. Fewer than had gone in their parents' time, and more than will go in our time now.

There is an honest ugliness that can warm the heart. Newborn babies, let it be whispered, are sometimes ugly, poignantly and tenderly ugly. I think of the grandfather in the well-known painting by Ghirlandaio, looking with kindly eyes upon his fresh-faced grandson. The old man boasts a nose clustered with warts. He is ugly in that honest way. My hometown in Pennsylvania was pocked with abandoned coal mines and great mounds of coal flakes, hundreds of feet high. I loved it. The old man in the painting says, "I am old, and I don't have a trace of my grandson's beauty. What of it?" The old town in my memory says, "I am old, and I bear the marks of a hundred years of hard work. What of it?" Such ugliness is real. It was no fantasy, that coal industry. They served no fantasy, those black diamonds the men hacked out of the earth, for trains to run, and for people to warm their stoves.

Then there is the ugly that is aggressive, expensive, and self-displaying. You must go well out of your way to attain it. It is like a body tattoo. Such was the ugliness of the whole halftime show, to which the football game was an appendage.

I recall the great moment in Robert Bolt's play *A Man for All Seasons*. Thomas More has been falsely accused of taking a bribe by Richard Rich, an ambitious little weasel of a man, and one whom More would not employ in any higher capacity than that of teacher. More's enemy Thomas Cromwell has made use of Rich as a perjured informant, rewarding him by making him attorney general for Wales. "Master Rich," says Thomas More, "it is said that it should little profit a man to gain the whole world and lose his own soul. *But for Wales?*"

For Wales? Wales was honest in its poverty, its wild mountains, its language so uncouth to English ears, and its passion for self-rule. The Great Stereopticon does not present us with Wales, not anymore. There hardly is such a Wales to present. The autobiographical novelist Richard Llewellyn and the director John Ford gave us that Wales, nearing its end, in *How Green Was My Valley* (1941). Only one out of six Welshmen now speaks *yr hen iaith*, the old tongue. Cardiff is an international city, which means, in our time, that it has no special character remaining. It is Seattle, only not as rainy.

The Stereopticon presents us with a fantasy, ugly, unsatisfying, uneasy, unsettling. Perhaps in this way it is more honest than it intends to be. For I note that almost every novel or play or film having to do with the distant future portrays it as ugly, unsatisfying, uneasy, unsettling, even inhuman. That would seem to run athwart the progressive notion that we are growing wiser and more enlightened by the hour. Our wise and enlightened descendants, if we are to take the assumedly dystopian Wales of the future as evidence, are the creatures that the Duke of Albany foresees, if such inhuman daughters of King Lear as the duke's wife Goneril should succeed in their political machinations:

> Humanity must perforce prey on itself,
> Like monsters of the deep.[4]

If Unreal is the city everyone wants to build, why does everyone imagine it as a place of darkness and despair?

[4] Shakespeare, *King Lear*, 4.2.50–51.

## Seeing Is Believing

I have sometimes wondered whether the most confused of our children, and of our fellow men and women in the world of Unreal, might rub their eyes, shake the film from their brains, and come to their senses, if they could only leave the idol factory behind for a few months, and go outdoors, do work that makes your flesh sweat and your bones ache with that good feeling of tiredness after a fruitful day, and feel your body for what it is rather than what you are instructed to imagine it to be. Elijah did not find God in the earthquake or the whirlwind or the fire but in the still, small voice. We do not have the advantages Elijah had. We have only bad dreams of earthquakes, whirlwinds, fires, and things more horrible still, and not one moment of peace to hear the voice of God.

It is not merely that the idol factory tells us false things about us and our world. We no longer know a world to have false things said about. The idol factory *is* the world. We do not judge between what the idol factory shows us and what we see with our eyes. The idol factory gives us our eyes. We are permitted to judge between idol and idol. We do not judge between idol and reality. No man or, now, woman can be elected the grand high mystic mayor of Unreal, if he were only to look us soberly in the eye and say, "Here is what the Constitution says, here is what our revenues are, these are our true needs, this is what we can afford, these are the moral hazards we run if we attempt to do this, these are the financial hazards we run if we attempt to do that", and so on. No one can become mayor of Unreal by looking squarely at the real. There is no real. It is all flash and glare, sound and fury. Hence the incessant polling that mars our politics: a hall of mirrors, each image reflecting itself in an infinite recess of reflections. We have polls about polls, and news about polls, and polls about news, and news about news, and there is not enough reality in the lot of it to get caught under a small boy's fingernail. I am not saying that the polls are inaccurate. They are terribly, horribly accurate. The puppet dances on the strings. Polls sell.

We believe what we see, and we see idols.

Consider the unreality of government in our time. We see Congress, we see the president, we even see people in lumpish black robes, whom we never used to have to look at, the justices of the Supreme Court. We see an elaborate game, a show of democracy, when the fact is that nobody knows the law of the land, unless he is a specialist in an exceedingly narrow portion of it. Nobody can know. Nobody knows who is responsible for the millions of regulations that press upon our lives. Nobody can know. It would be like knowing the action of every protein in every cell of an animal's body, with this difference: we can know the animal, because it is a natural creature with well-observed habits and instincts. We cannot know Unreal. It is not a natural creature. It is Hobbes' Leviathan, perhaps. Nobody knows it. Nobody can put a ring in its nose.

I can make the point more clearly, perhaps, by inflating the scale a little further. Suppose, instead of a government of 325 million people, you had a government of 325 millions of millions of people. Suppose, instead of encompassing three million square miles on a single planet, it encompassed three millions of three million square miles on a million planets. And then suppose you said, "Ah, but we govern ourselves, because every four years we get to vote for the interplanetary president, along with our votes for interplanetary Congress; and the president nominates and the interplanetary Senate confirms our nine interplanetary cultural archons, called the Supreme Interplanetary Court." Self-government, to be sure. People are free not because they get to cast a marked piece of confetti for their distant rulers but because their distant rulers have only very distant things to do with them, if anything at all. Liberty is to be defined not by how many things you or your representatives get to vote about, with your own vote so diluted that it would be like a grain of sand in the Sahara desert, but rather by how many things no one needs to vote about, or no one dares to vote about, because they get done by ordinary people pursuing their own good and the common good in ordinary ways.

The political is, in our time, eminently the realm of the unreal, and it is all the more unreal in that it looms enormous in our vision—Jabba the State, if I may steal an image from another of the Stereopticon's slides. Political speeches have always been prone to Boyle's Law of gases: they fill the empty heads that take them in. But we no longer have speeches, properly speaking. We have commercials. Everything is a commercial. When a senator questions a witness, he is not asking for information. He is adopting a pose, because he knows the cameras are on him. The State of the Union address is not a State of the Union address, that is, a report by the chief executive officer to a board of trustees. It is a commercial. In 2019 the liberal women elected to Congress decided to make a big display of themselves, dressing up in virginal white, which was a little as if Hitler decided to sport a yarmulke; nothing but a commercial. Charlie Chaplin already saw, in *The Great Dictator* (1940), that a man like Hitler could come to power through Chaplin's own medium.

It is a sobering thought to recall the televised Kennedy-Nixon debate in 1960, which those who watched the images on television believed that Kennedy had won, while those who only heard it on the radio believed that Nixon had won. Nixon had had the flu, and looked gaunt, badly shaven, and haggard, while Kennedy had that characteristic slightly pudgy boyishness about him. Now, of course, we judge the "winner" of a political debate in much the same way as the judges on *American Idol* cast ballots for the contending performers. There is no substance, or even style, but only the show of style. Women, quicker to seize upon a visual cue for sociability, and more emotionally suggestible, will now react against any candidate, male or female, who might dare, in a dry, satirical, fact-heavy, logically unexceptionable, and utterly devastating way, to dismember an idol of the time, whether the idol is imaginary or is sitting across from him and running for office. When the brain is saturated with pornographic images, then the pretty girl in a comely dress, sitting across from you on the train, might as well be a bag of potatoes. When the flesh crawls with the political hives, you have not the patience or the concentration to analyze an argument. There are no arguments, then. There are no debates. There are only commercials, and people judge the effectiveness of the commercial in the same way they might judge the force of an itch. Hence the "focus group", to report to pollsters its dermal responses.

We might put it this way too. A fat man like Grover Cleveland or William Howard Taft could not now become president. An ugly man like John Quincy Adams, Abraham Lincoln, or William McKinley could not now become president. A man with a forbidding personality, apparently distant and calculating, like Calvin Coolidge or James Polk, could not now become president. Men of incisive intellect who have written controversial things, such as James Madison or Theodore Roosevelt, could not now become president. Toys and toymakers can become president.

## The Fanaticized Consciousness

I do not mean to suggest, above, that mass man engaging in mass politics becomes merely brutalized, mere flesh and no mind. In a sense, as I have been trying to show, he loses his flesh in abstraction: all things, including himself, become ideations, and as such they are easily manipulable by the mass phenomena. So it is not John who votes but an ideation of John, John as a representative of abstracted categories; and the politicians, themselves little more than mummies in action, appeal not to John but to the categories.

Gabriel Marcel, in *Man against Mass Society* (1952), discusses just this turn from the individual person to the unit in the mass and says that it is a feature of the "fanaticized consciousness", a thing that might well set one to brooding, after the rise of Adolf Hitler. Why, he asks, is mass man so easily permeated by the fanatical?

> The individual, in order to belong to the mass, to be a mass-man, has had, as a preliminary, though without having had the least awareness of it, to divest himself of that substantial reality which was linked to his initial individuality or rather to the fact of his belonging to a small actual group. The incredibly sinister role of the press, the cinema, the radio, has consisted in passing that original reality through a pair of flattening rollers to substitute for it a superimposed pattern of ideas and images with no real roots in the deep being of the subject of this experiment. But does it not seem just as if propaganda offered a kind of nourishment to the unconscious hunger felt by beings thus deprived of their own proper reality?[5]

[5] Gabriel Marcel, "The Fanaticized Consciousness", in *Man against Mass Society*, trans. G. S. Fraser (Chicago: Regnery, 1962; first published in English, 1952), p. 141.

Let us tease this out a little. I am an ordinary human being
—let us say, a man who raises pigs in upstate New York, as
did my wife's uncle Willard. He used to get up very early
every morning, because the pigs were not moved by the supposedly great events in Washington, London, and Moscow.
They needed to be watered and fed. The cows needed to
be seen to also, and milked, lest their udders grow painful.
The boar in the field and the chickens in the field—they too
did not care one whit for the Federal Reserve or the World
Bank. Aunt Ruth too must be up and about, because when
Willard came back in the house after a couple of hours of
work, he was going to be ferociously hungry.

There used to be children in the house, and they had
their early morning chores, unless it was a school day, in
which case they trudged off to meet the bus. Everyone was
embedded in a real community. The cow chews her cud,
no matter who is on the television, and the bull snorts and
rakes the earth. No one thinks of himself as a counter in
a vast, mainly invisible, and strangely unreal group. There
are animals, crops, fields, families, a couple of villages, two
or three churches, earth and tree and rock and sky.

There is also what medieval Englishmen called "neighborhood", naming not a geographical area but a virtue, correlative with "brotherhood". You live among neighbors,
and you put up with them and do for them, and sometimes
your son marries the neighbor's daughter. J. R. R. Tolkien's
"Leaf, by Niggle" illustrates the virtue in a way that seems
inconceivable to us now. It is one thing, perhaps, to make a
telephone call for the man who lives nearby when his wife
has a cold. It is another thing to do so when you do not even
care much for the fellow. It is still another to do what Niggle does, which is to ride his bicycle into town, in the rain,
to fetch the doctor, because the neighbor, the aptly named

Parish, is lame; and that is not because Niggle is a saint, or because he loves his neighbors—he is mainly irritated with them, because Parish has no sense of what the artist Niggle does, and Niggle has no sense of Parish's hobby, gardening. He does it because that is what neighbors do. And he does it with a grumble.

No such thing will happen now. You have no neighbors, my dear readers. Or you have only a few; the others are simply people whose houses are situated within a reasonable proximity to your own. Your "city" is rather like Anchorage, Alaska. I do not mean that the weather is cold. The climate of Anchorage is mild, and I imagine that the people are friendly enough. It is that Anchorage spans an area almost twice as large as the state of Rhode Island. Such a city is a fiction. It is a fiction that robs people in villages far from the nuclear city, taking from them their authority to see to their common needs by themselves. Your school district is a fiction. It is a fiction that robs people who live in what used to be a neighborhood with a neighborhood school, taking from them their authority to run such a school according to their lights. Almost every political entity is now a fiction. The leaders of nations seem bent upon transforming or unforming them, making them fictional also—a Germany that is no longer German, populated by semicitizens who speak German but who have no care for the German heritage of religious faith, literature, and art, and by other semicitizens who speak German for convenience and who also have no care for that heritage. The European Union is a fiction. For nothing has ever united Europe but the Christian faith, and the officials of that self-styled union regularly deny the faith. People are not united by a common currency—which is itself a fiction, backed up by nothing of enduring value.

What can happen when man has no roots, no such "proper reality", as Marcel calls it? Man's nature abhors the vacuum:

Propaganda will thus create a kind of second and entirely factitious nature, but a nature which can only be sustained and kept alive by a passion, by, in fact, precisely the passion of fanaticism. We ought certainly to add here that the basis of this passion is fear, that it implies an unconfessed emotional insecurity that converts itself into an outward aggressiveness. It is by the existence of this secret fear that we can most conveniently explain the refusal, involved in all types of fanaticism, to bring basic assumptions into question.[6]

Let me as always give examples. The man who thinks that America is the pinnacle of man's social achievement cannot abide the suggestion that his republic might have been founded upon false principles. The feminist cannot abide the suggestion that the interests of the sexes, as Mrs. Schuyler Van Rensselaer wrote in *Should We Ask for the Suffrage?* (1894), are not separable, and that to say that women needed to look out for themselves was a slander to American men, "who have so cordially helped us to become the freest and most highly considered women in the world".[7] The black activist cannot abide the suggestion that the black family was healthier in the days of Jim Crow than it is now, though that is nothing to the credit of Jim Crow, and all to the blame of the individualism in matters of sex that we have so foolishly and so heartlessly pursued. The man who believes that the world is going to fry in its own increasing heat will turn on you like a wolverine if you ask how he

[6] Ibid.
[7] Mrs. Schuyler Van Rensselaer, *Should We Ask for the Suffrage?* (n.p., [1894]), p. 57, https://archive.org/details/shouldweaskforsu00vanruoft.

can be certain of that, or even how he knows that a slightly warmer global climate will not be a good thing, all in all. The gay activist will attack you for your "hate" if you suggest that there is no such thing as *being* gay, but there are only men and women, with good or bad habits as the case may be. We say that a man "is" a thief, if he steals things, but we do not say that he "is" a thief essentially. He may have powerful urges to steal things, but his urges do not determine what he is, nor are they completely independent of what he chooses to do. I can understand why John might stop speaking to his brother James if James knowingly sold him a car that broke down. I cannot understand why he might stop speaking to James if James persuaded him to vote for a lousy politician.

I do not want to suggest that fanaticism is wholly a feature of the political Left. There are Catholics who hate the Novus Ordo Mass more than they love the Tridentine rite they attend. There is no Savior for man but Jesus, and the Christian faith is in a Person, not an idea, nor even in a Person as embodying an idea. But that tendency toward abstraction has been characteristic of liberal Christianity, thus. The Christian loses faith in the Divine Person of Jesus, and he turns instead to a supposed divine Idea that Jesus fully personifies. In the next phase, Jesus himself is slightly dislocated from that Idea, so that he personifies it in the way that Socrates, for Plato, personified the ideal life of the mind; Jesus is now the best of teachers, merely. We fall from there to admiring Jesus for being a very fine teacher, but what he teaches is itself to be judged by the degree to which it is in harmony with an Idea we have arrived at, independent of him. This Idea might, in earlier times, have been formed by the mind's encounter with such things as the mystic philosophy of Plotinus. In these times, it is not so. The Idea is

a contemporary fiction. It is the product of the mass phenomena. It is itself propaganda.

"I am the vine, ye are the branches", said Jesus (Jn 15:5),
and that is the inner meaning of "propagation": you send
out new shoots, and the shoots all bear the characteristics of
the parent vine. But propaganda, as mass man experiences
it, engages in it, and suffers it, is like branches without a
vine. We do not propagate the faith. We instead have faith
in propaganda. The true faith loses its urgency. Philip sought
Nathanael and fairly cried out to him, "We have found him,
of whom Moses in the law, and the prophets, did write, Jesus
of Nazareth, the son of Joseph" (Jn 1:45). Come and see! It
was to meet the man, in the flesh, who would become the
center of your life, because he is the one through whom all
things have been made. When we deny the reality, shadows
and shows then become urgent to us. "Hate has no place
here", say the signs, without a trace of self-awareness or
irony. Look at the faces of people marching for a political
cause. If they are contorted in wrath, accusatory, drawn in
fear when there is nothing to fear, adopting a hideousness
to which even fallen man is not born, then you know that
you are at an Unreal Bastille, where man storms his fellow
man, or where simulacra of men storm simulacra of men.
Only fanaticism can sustain it.


## All Brain and Belly, No Chest

One might think that at least our intellectual institutions
would be guardians against politics as show, and the fanaticism that it requires and breeds. One might think.

There is a fanaticism in a kind of logic detached from
the good corporal realities of human life. It begins in hatred

or disdain, usually disdain for what men have always and everywhere thought to be good and decent. It ends in utter unreason. Says Arthur Koestler, in *Darkness at Noon* (1941):

> Satan, on the contrary, is thin, ascetic and a fanatical devotee of logic. He reads Machiavelli, Ignatius of Loyola, Marx and Hegel; he is cold and unmerciful to mankind, out of a kind of mathematical mercifulness. He is damned always to do that which is most repugnant to him: to become a slaughterer, in order to abolish slaughtering, to sacrifice lambs so that no more lambs may be slaughtered, to whip people with knouts so that they may learn not to let themselves be whipped, to strip himself of every scruple in the name of a higher scrupulousness, and to challenge the hatred of mankind because of his love for it—an abstract and geometric love.[8]

That is the vicious circle of the modern liberal. The pose can be cool, even arctic. Political philosopher John Rawls is the archpriest of the pose. He asks us—nay, he demands it of us, under pain of banishment from civic discourse—that we pretend that we are not sons and daughters, fathers and mothers, husbands and wives, neighbors and members of a community, in *this place* and not another, worshiping God in this church and in these ways, and devoted to a certain vision of the good, a vision that we do not deduce from abstract principles but either see intuitively or experience in the blood. He requires us, in short, not to be human at all, and only then, or only insofar as we can adopt the pose of the bloodless and desiccated, may we come together to form a contract, a profoundly antisocial contract, dictating civil rights, punishments, rewards, and so forth.

---

[8] Arthur Koestler, *Darkness at Noon*, trans. Daphne Hardy (New York: Macmillan, 1941), p. 122.

The results parade themselves as universally valid, and they do exactly what Rawls, to give him the benefit of the doubt, did not want. He did not want the powerful in any society to rig the machine to confirm their power. Everyone is supposed to cloak himself in a veil of ignorance, so that we will not know whom the contract will benefit and in what ways. What we end up with is what Richard John Neuhaus famously called "the naked public square". It is bleached of religious commitment, and of almost all piety, broadly understood to include your duty to your country and your forefathers. It is favorable to those whose devotion to places and specific persons is thin. It recognizes no natural polities anterior to the contract: families, then, are demoted to choices among "lifestyles", itself a word straight from the Unreal marketplace. It is favorable to clever and well-heeled hedonists, who are good at balancing sexual pleasure, money, prestige, and power. It produces, we might say, a government *by* Yale law students, *for* Yale law students, thrust upon people whom Yale law students patronize.

It is hedonism in sexual matters, and statism in everything else: the combination that characterizes Huxley's *Brave New World*. A dreadful combination. And I think that its promoters, who benefit from it handsomely, understand deep down that it is dreadful; they probably suspect that our supine acceptance of mores that eviscerate the poor, robbing them of their only fund of capital, which is moral and familial, has been calamitous for the very people they purport to assist. Hence the frenetic desire, almost a psychological compulsion, to lay blame somewhere, anywhere; to see in innocent people a racism they do not feel, and to magnify human inclinations, good or bad, into a vast and vague "structure", a "system" of evil—a structure without posts and lintels you can grasp, a system without laws or lawgivers you can name.

I do not say that ordinary people are free of bad habits or inclinations, or that they are entirely fair to people around them. That is not fallen man. But I do not require ordinary people to be saints on earth. They never will be so. I require them only to be half-decent. And in that regard I will freely admit that good laws are for the making of good men.

More on that in a moment. I have suggested that the show of dispassionate logic in political matters is mainly that— a show. We can see it most clearly when we draw near to a sacred idol and dare to pick it up, turn it upside-down, scratch its surface, and smell the rust that has eaten into its vitals. I will mention two such idols here. One is *consent.*

"You clearly do not understand the theory of consent", said a young person to me. He was defending the disgraceful treatment that the dispassionate reasoners at Yale had visited upon conservative law students, who had invited to campus a representative of the Alliance Defending Freedom. The ADF is a "hate group", according to the odium-monitors of the Southern Poverty Law Center, because its members do not subscribe to the notion that a man can feasibly marry another man. Ah, but I do understand the theory of consent, I replied. I reject it.

Consent is a liberal talisman. It is supposed to make everything all right. Of course it does not, and nobody really believes that it does. I asked my interlocutor to take one step away from his preferred realm of the consensual. Duelists consent. People playing Russian roulette consent. Men at a high-stakes private poker game consent. Bigamists consent. The loan shark and his mark consent. Consent in evil is, in one sense, worse than compulsion. It is a veritable conspiracy.

There are two ready replies. One is that dueling harms somebody, and so it is not analogous to, say, fornication, which has no consequences whatsoever, either for the man and woman involved or the child they may conceive. When you put it that way, you see the absurdity in an instant. People can say that their preferred method of obtaining pleasure does not harm anybody, only if from the outset they limit very severely what shall qualify as harm, and only if they do not trouble to ask about the universalizing effects that follow from their principal cause. The man who says that he is not harming anybody when he strips naked on a public beach has begged the whole question: he has simply ruled out of consideration all those harms that his indecency brings about. That many people then will not want to go to that beach, especially with their children, is so much the better for him.

The other reply touches upon the second of the idols I have in mind, that of *equality*. It is to say that bigamy, for instance, or perhaps prostitution, does not imply true and full consent, because those things involve a differential in power: the husband over his wives, the first wife over the second wife, and the pimp and the customer over the whore.

But I do not see that this is the case, nor do I see why it should matter. A man with two wives may find himself henpecked twice over. The young wife may lady it over the older wife, just because she is younger, more energetic, and more fruitful. The prostitute may bleed a man dry. But why should someone not desire the subordinate position? Other than that all right-thinking graduates of Yale are supposed to believe in consent and equality, why should one not want the pleasures of inequality? Between existence and nonexistence lies a fathomless chasm of inequality. If the same graduates of Yale believe that one can rationally choose the infinitely lesser of those two, and even in some cases compel a physician to provide that final push into emptiness, then, a fortiori, what can they possibly have against the duelists and the bigamists and the loan shark and his clientele? If we can responsibly choose death, why not then life under compulsion? The younger wife gets to make the bedsprings squeak, the losing duelist has defended his honor, and the prodigal has money to burn for another month. Two of them at least are not dead, and the duelist may recover from his wounds.

And what really is the force of consent, for the hedonistic intelligentsia? They scoff at people who follow a religious tradition that is twenty centuries old and that spans the world, while they follow a social and intellectual fad that is twenty years old and that is peculiar to their class.

## Bridges Too Far

It is a truism in Unreal City that if there is one thing you cannot legislate about, it is morality. That is like saying that if there is one thing an actor cannot portray, it is a man in a situation. Let me address questions of morality in what are always going to be areas of contention: money and sex.

Because I try to be an orthodox Catholic, taking my inspiration from the teachings of the Church, I cannot be a libertarian; nor do I think that libertarians have much that is useful to say about the fulfillment of man's nature as a social being. I also suspect, in my moments of sporadic agreement with the pacifist theologian Stanley Hauerwas, that we Christians in the United States have a greater need of beggars than we would care to admit. We need people who turn aside from the moneying game. Some of those beggars may be unemployable for practical reasons, but others may be genuine contemplatives, who remind us that the heart of life is not to be found in a paycheck or in the fancy things we snatch at the store.

Charles Dickens, who had a Low Church suspicion against anything remotely suggestive of the monastic, as witnessed by the name he gave to the soul-cramped village in *Edwin Drood*—Cloisterham—seems to have longed for a way to combine responsible business with detachment from goods as such: think of the elderly banker Jarvis Lorry in *A Tale of Two Cities*, or the Cheeruble Brothers in *Nicholas Nickleby*. Not entirely successful, these portrayals. Dickens had no affection for people who made money for money's sake, but he did admire, with his mind if not his heart, men who could make things that work. And he saw through the pretensions of the prodigal and the irresponsible. So we have Mr. Micawber in *David Copperfield*, whose family is always on the verge of destitution while he waits for "something to turn up", and the practitioner of "telescopic philanthropy", Mrs. Jellyby, who in her protofeminist social justice warrior way spends her hours getting people to subscribe for a charitable trade in coffee and missionary work with the natives of Borioboola-Gha, while her own flat is a wreck and her children ill tended and dirty and her husband abandoned. The poor are to be loved and assisted, but that does not mean that they are always innocent or admirable or even spiritually detached from the riches they do not have. It is harder for a poor man than a rich man to be consumed with avarice. It is not impossible.

Nor do I have any natural affection for rich people. The small town where I grew up had a few sort-of rich people in it: the family that owned the oldest continuously running pharmacy in the country (now defunct); the family of the town doctor; the family that ran the town's biggest grocery store (now a supermarket, sold away). I went to the local Catholic grade school with the children from these families, who lived pretty much as everyone else lived, except that their houses were bigger. My first real encounter with Money came when I went to Princeton and met young people who went to boarding schools (what were they?), whose parents took vacations to Bermuda (we went to visit my cousins in New Jersey), whose pastimes included sailing (our Lackawanna River was four feet deep), and who frequented expensive restaurants (we could get lobster at Sharkey's for three dollars a pound). I found it hard sometimes to make friends with them, not that I or they tried very hard at it.

So I do not exactly sympathize with "the rich", whoever they may be, but I do not envy them, either, and I certainly do not want their money. They can keep it, for all I care, and for all the good it will do them. There is something that unsettles me about the idea that they "owe" me or their country a far greater portion of their substance than I or anybody else owes. I understand that, within reason, rich people should pay taxes in accordance with their wealth, and so they do. But I want to be careful here. If a bridge needs to be built, then the state has the moral duty to raise money to build the bridge, which will serve the common good. It is justifiable, then, and one can make a case for it, to tax wealthy people at a somewhat higher rate than others are taxed, to build the bridge; for it may be that the wealthy will enjoy a greater benefit from anything that the state does to encourage trade or business, seeing that they have more substance to invest in business to begin with.

Bridges have the fine advantage of being real things. I often drive a car over one of them. And when the politicians of Unreal demand more money for their designs and their lives, they always bring up the Bridge. No one says, because even in Unreal no one would believe it, that we the government of Unreal require more money because our middle management, ever expanding, cannot do its work efficiently, whatever that work may be, without higher salaries and a greater number of positions. Yet the people of Unreal can be moved to want to soak the rich, because the rich are made to be soaked, trusting that, by some magic of welfare law, some sweet drops of that wealth will trickle down upon their heads.

I want to live in a real place. Real places bring forth real expectations, to meet real needs. So it does not seem right to me to advocate taking money from Smith, because he has it, to give it to Jones, because he does not have it, without making Jones subject to expectations enjoined upon him by the local community of which Smith or someone like Smith is a part. That is, if I lend money to my nephew Ronnie, I have the right to expect that he will not blow it at a casino but will use it for the purpose for which I lent it. That is not simply because it was *my money* but because I could have put that same money to a hundred other uses. I might have given it instead to my niece or my neighbor. I might have done real and immediately human things with it.

The principle is similar to that of eminent domain. The state may take my property, compensating me for it with a just price, to build something that might, in principle, be used by everyone, directly or nearly directly, such as a bridge, a road, a harbor, or an airport. But it may not in justice take my property merely to give it to someone else, like a developer, who happens to want it and who dangles in front of the city the possibility of a higher tax base. I might want to keep my house for selfish reasons, just as a miser might want to keep his money. But I might want to keep it for good and generous reasons, just as a father who has been successful in business might use some of his wealth to build a neighborhood playground, or to set up a family member in a trade, or to buy new hymnals for his church.

The welfare state begins by compelling people to put money aside for their old age—the unreality of the Social Security trust fund comes to mind. There, at least, there is some correspondence between what the state takes from you and what the state will give back. And the state has a genuine interest in keeping people from destitution. But what happens eventually is that people in charge of a welfare state come to think of all things as belonging to them. The unreality goes to the brain. Children, for instance, are wards of the state, lent out to their parents conditionally; families are creations of the state; money is all the state's to play with, so that if Senator Phogbound refrains from raising the taxes of Mr. Yokum, he may be regarded as having done him a good turn. So the man waiting for the bus should thank the pickpocket for having idle fingers for once. Nor do I see that Death should be some game-scrambler, the great opportunity to ignore the generation-spanning essence of the family, so as to rifle half an estate, often compelling people to sell a homestead just to pay the taxes on it.

Until recently, most thinkers about justice have assumed not only that laws should reflect and promote what is morally good, and punish evil, but that good laws helped to make their subjects better. Customs, too, perform much of the work of law, and usually with far greater efficacy, for good and for bad. In Unreal, you cannot bring these things up without being accused of hatred. But I have sometimes considered how some dubious customs, and bad or weak laws, have long thwarted the economic development of that part of the world from which my ancestors came: southern Italy, the chief culture analyzed by Edward Banfield in *The Moral Basis of a Backward Society* (1958).

Banfield saw that the economic backwardness—if we assume that in fact it is a better thing to be industrial Milan than crime-ridden Naples, and I am not entirely sure that I want to give the nod to Milan without further consideration of what family life is like in both places—depends not so much upon political ideology or even natural resources but upon morals. It was the same kind of cold-eyed analysis that led him, in *The Unheavenly City* (1970), to entitle one of his chapters on American cities in the 1960s "Looting for Fun and Profit".

Here we might engage in a nice thought experiment, asking, "What would happen to people's honesty, and to business in general, if we treated contracts with the same insouciance with which we treat the marriage vow?" A marriage is a marriage contract but not a business contract. The adulterer can walk away with half the assets. If the embezzler in a business partnership is caught doing that, he ends up in jail. The laws encourage honesty in money matters mainly by punishing dishonesty. Is that, then, the only area of law that the citizens of Unreal will acknowledge as instructive of morality?

No, not really. Sometimes Unreal is happily inconsistent. It has occurred to me that there is one group in America that has been, perhaps inadvertently, conceding the point, that good laws not only reward good behavior but encourage it, and help people to become good. Who are they? The male homosexuals arguing for the right to "marry".

Anyone who has paid attention to the self-described lives of homosexual men must be struck by the mind-boggling promiscuity; and this promiscuity, sometimes in the form of group events, is a matter-of-course part of the homosexual life. Yet, as the argument went, such promiscuity was not simply the result of the desires of homosexual men themselves. It was also, it was said, the result of their inability to form legally binding marriages. If marriage were available to them—a biological absurdity, but let's ignore that for the present—then not only would that recognize and reward those men who would have devoted their lives faithfully to one another in any case, but it would encourage other men to do the same. It would restrain the promiscuity; it would change the world of the homosexual male.

Now, I never did believe that the marriage go-ahead would achieve these effects to any significant degree, because I did not believe that the relations of male homosexuals were analogous to the relations of married men and women. In Unreal, bodies matter for your indefinable sense of identity but not for anything else; marriage and even the fundamental realities of male and female dissolve in the acid soup of desire. But the world does not obey the laws of Unreal.

From what I have read and from what homosexual men themselves have told me, it seems that the relations are sexualizations of male friendships, and friendship is a different thing—not necessarily a greater or even a lesser thing but a different thing—from what men and women experience when they give themselves to one another in marriage. Still, I would like to note the presumption of the argument. It was not, "People will do whatever they do, sexually, regardless of the law." It was, "Laws can make people better, not just by deterring the bad, but by encouraging and teaching the good." People who make this argument assume, tacitly, that it would be a good thing if the relationships of male homosexuals were more permanent, and since they would not be more permanent if the men involved did not want them to be so, we must conclude that the goodness includes the *desire*, now made more frequent, of the men to form permanent relationships. In other words, the tacit assumption is not simply that a law permitting male-male pseudogamy would be just but that it would make many of the men themselves more virtuous.

And that, dear readers, gives the game away. We may then argue—we must argue—about what in sexual matters is good and bad, what will make us a more virtuous or a more vicious people, what we seek to affirm in marriage, what is good or bad for a child to see as allowable behavior, what we look for from manhood and womanhood, and so forth. We may not simply assume that people are inert and utterly invariable from time to time and culture to culture. That is not real. We do have the right to ask, "What kind of society will this law help to produce?" And, "What virtues —or vices—will this law or custom help to teach?"

## Rah, Rah, Rah!

It follows that people cannot answer those questions above, or even understand that they are to be asked, unless they are grounded in human realities. That is why Aristotle, in the *Nicomachean Ethics*, says that "a young man is not a proper hearer of lectures on political science; for he is inexperienced in the actions that occur in life, but its discussions start from these and are about these; and, further, since he tends to follow his passions, his study will be vain and unprofitable, because the end aimed at is not knowledge but action." But in Unreal, as we have seen, the young are fairly pitched into political fever. Or I should say pseudopolitical, because the young have very little experience with the common life of free men and women. They are all in a lather for shows, as people adopt a favorite baseball club, except that nobody would kill over a rivalry between the Cardinals and the Cubs.

Or would they? In the reign of Justinian, in 532, riots broke out in Constantinople between the Greens and the Blues, partisans of different teams of chariot racers. The sporting partisans had begun to dig themselves in also as partisans of certain political and theological positions. Hatreds erupted into bloodshed everywhere, nearly toppling the emperor himself.

A strange phenomenon. It is hard to say whether the Greens and the Blues sought to murder each other because their religion had gotten infected with the irrational passions of sport and simulated war, or whether their sport and simulated war had gotten infected with religious zealotry. What interests me here is that whichever way you look at it, it appears that the *vehicle* for the rioting was the game, the let's-pretend of the chariot races. The game is a good thing, if we understand that it is a game. I do not mean to say that it is *just* a game: for the best of games assist us by reflecting reality itself, or by suspending our hasty judgments so that we can ourselves reflect upon reality more deeply. Hence liturgy is, so to speak, a game of worship: again, not *just* a game but the serious work of play and prayer, the solemn and often joyful work of the holy day.

It is when the game becomes utterly detached from a founding in reality that it can grow pathological. For the sake of the game, we pretend that our players are good and their opponents are bad, and it is the task of the good to defeat the bad. But we know that it is not really so, and we can imagine ourselves into the roles of the fans on the opposite side, who believe that their players are good and ours are bad. Then we can appreciate the courage, skill, perseverance, and cunning of the enemy as qualities that are good in themselves.

And the effects run in the other direction too. If the game is a simulated war, war can sometimes and in a healthy way be regarded as a most earnest game. William Sherman was severely criticized by his enemies in Congress, who were doubtless spurred on by envious officers in the Union Army, for allowing generous terms of surrender to Confederate soldiers. That was not because Sherman was a kindly man. He burned that broad swath from Atlanta to the sea, ripping up railroad ties and destroying everything in sight, to break the economic back of the Confederacy. "War is hell", said Sherman. But it seems also that war for him was the game of war. Its quality as a game granted to Sherman the capacity to see himself as more like to the generals on the other side than either would be to the politicians. Livy casts Hannibal as disdainful of the Carthaginian Senate, and when the wily fellow speaks to Scipio before the decisive battle of Zama, it is as one soldier to another, who understand one another because they are the players, while the politicians are spectators or profiteers. So when Sherman's erstwhile enemy, General Joseph E. Johnston, served as Sherman's pallbearer at his funeral in New York, on a day that was cold and rainy, the former Confederate, now a man of eighty-four years, insisted upon wearing no hat, as a sign of respect. "If I were in his place," said Johnston, "and he were standing in mine, he would not put on his hat."[9] Johnston caught a bad cold from that day and died several weeks later.

Men who are balanced can use the play, the game, to reveal reality: "The play's the thing", says Hamlet, "wherein I'll

[9] Craig L. Symonds, *Joseph E. Johnston: A Civil War Biography* (New York: W. W. Norton, 1992), pp. 380–81.

catch the conscience of the king."[10] And in some sense they retain a healthy skepticism about the other games that men play. They understand that the games are not the ultimate thing. But in our time the games of politics, especially with regard to sex and, it appears, race, have supplanted reality, so that it is difficult for people to hold important truths in mind at once: that people are of a middling virtue at best; that our knowledge is incomplete and often shot through with distortions and errors; and that the world will go on as it is, regardless of what we say about it. We buy the urgency; we allow ourselves to be embroiled in the political, as if the whole terrifying power of the sexual, of the instinct to preserve our lives, and, especially, of the mother's ferocious drive to protect her young were hinging upon the next vote in the Senate, or upon whether a certain state goes Blue or Green in the next off-year election. It is electoral dysfunction of a painful and insufferable sort: tumescent without issue, and with no relief in sight.

[10] Shakespeare, *Hamlet*, 2.2.611–12.

# 4

# The Spiritual Chasm

It is fashionable in progressive Christian circles to decry the notion that there might be a hell. I will not enter here into the theological arguments surrounding universal salvation. I wish to specify only what it is we are affirming or denying. When in the beginning God made the heavens and the earth, says the sacred author, "the earth was without form, and void" (Gen 1:2), in Hebrew *tohu w'vohu*, a fine rhyming pair, and the first figure of speech in Scripture. The words suggest inanity, nonbeing. *Vohu* in fact is used only as a rhyme for *tohu*, never otherwise, and the pair is used also to describe what idols are. It is not simply that the gods are false. They are inane. They are without meaning.

Evil, says Augustine, is not a thing in itself but an absence, a vacuity. Moral evil is a freely willed turn toward that vacuity. Milton's Moloch fairly gives the secret away when, among the assembled devils newly damned and pretending to meet to figure out a way to recoup their losses, he recommends armed rebellion against the Almighty. His war cry begins in bravado and ends in a hope for nothingness. If the Almighty should defeat them again? Moloch seems almost to long for that to happen:

> More destroyed than thus,
> We should be quite abolished, and expire.
> What fear we then? What doubt we to incense

His utmost ire? Which to the height enraged
Will either quite consume us, and reduce
To nothing this essential, happier far
Than miserable to have eternal being;
Or if our substance be indeed divine
And cannot cease to be, we are at worst
On this side nothing.[1]

His sentiments are echoed later on by Satan, who can no
more escape from hell by change of place than he can escape
from himself and from the emptiness within him:

Me miserable! Which way shall I fly
Infinite wrath, or infinite despair?
Which way I fly is Hell; myself am Hell,
And in the lowest deep a lower deep
Still threatening to devour me opens wide,
To which the Hell I suffer seems a Heaven.[2]

"How comes it, then, that thou art out of hell?" says Doctor
Faustus to the tempter Mephistophilis, in Marlowe's play.
"Why this is hell nor am I out of it", says the devil in reply.[3]

We are asking here whether the rational soul can freely
choose to attempt to step out of being: to choose the vacuity, and to continue to choose it, attempting to stuff its
emptiness with emptiness. When the question is asked in
that fashion, we sense, with some terror, that the answer is
certainly yes. Satan, says Jesus, "was a murderer from the
beginning, and abode not in the truth, because there is no
truth in him. When he speaketh a lie, he speaketh of his
own: for he is a liar, and the father of it" (Jn 8:44). Satan is

[1] John Milton, *Paradise Lost*, 2.92–101.

[2] Ibid., 4.73–78.

[3] *Doctor Faustus*, ed. Paul Menzer (London: Methuen Drama, 2019), act 1,
scene 3, lines 72–73.

not merely a murderer and a liar both. He murders because
he lies: to lie, in essence, is to give yourself up to the unreal.
It is pure negation: it would return the world to its original
chaos. It is to attempt to put being itself to death. It is thus a
chilling coincidence that the English Germanic word "hell"
is cognate with "hollow": a place defined by absence. The
soul committed to the lie not only may be sent to hell; that
soul longs for hell. As the cowardly Belial says, in his riposte
to Moloch:

> What when we fled amain, pursued and strook
> By heaven's afflicting thunder, and besought
> The deep to shelter us? This hell then seemed
> A refuge from those wounds.[4]

In *The Great Divorce* (1945), C. S. Lewis, taking his cue
from Milton and Dante, portrays hell not only as a vast,
endlessly fissionable, gray city below, ever extending into
emptier and emptier suburbs, but as being able to fit inside
a crack in the real world, a crack so small as to be virtually
invisible. It is why the souls granted a respite from that city,
and a chance to repent and be made whole again, experience the blades of grass in the lovely borderlands of heaven
as pointed and sharp, like swords. Reality is too real for our
half-alive souls. Reality pierces, like a lance.

## See No Evil, Hear No Evil, Speak No Evil

That diagnostician of political unreality, Eric Voegelin, says
that we can tell that a man or a movement or a nation
has turned resolutely toward nonbeing when certain questions are disallowed from the beginning. For man's view is

[4] Milton, *Paradise Lost*, 2.165–68.

Dante

partial and his pragmatic settlements are provisional. Hence, he must heed those who see more than he does, who have committed themselves to the contemplation of the order of being as a whole. Philosophy then is most itself, and most beneficial to man, when it causes him to take stock of himself and his situation at every pass, and when it confronts a partial truth with another truth. Says Voegelin, in *Science, Politics, and Gnosticism*:

> When impetuous young men are repelled by the vulgarity of democracy, Plato can point out to them that energy, pride, and will to rule can indeed establish the despotism of a spiritually corrupt elite, but not a just government; and when democrats rave about freedom and equality and forget that government requires spiritual training and intellectual discipline, he can warn them that they are on the way to tyranny.[5]

What most oppresses man is not physical but spiritual, that is, an attack not on a particular political stance but on the very notion of truth itself: "The opposition becomes truly radical and dangerous only when philosophical questioning is itself called into question, when *doxa* [opinion] takes on the appearance of philosophy, when it arrogates to itself the name of science and prohibits science as nonscience."[6]

For "science" here, understand "pursuit of and possession of knowledge", not to be limited to the methods and the results of empirical and quantifiable measurements of the material world.

Every question you can imagine enters the field for Thomas Aquinas, including such foundational questions as whether theology is a field of knowledge at all, and whether

[5] Eric Voegelin, *Science, Politics and Gnosticism* (Wilmington, Del.: ISI Books, 2007), p. 14.

[6] Ibid., p. 15.

God, the subject of theological discourse, exists. But in hell, and in those human enterprises that partake of the character of hell, there are certain questions that must never be asked. They would reecho through all the chasms of unmeaning. Not one of the fallen angels in *Paradise Lost* dares to ask the obvious question, "Why should we continue to follow the leader who has brought us to destruction?" They fear to ask it; they flatter Satan instead, performing in bodily gesture a kind of self-annihilating obeisance that the supposed Tyrant in heaven never exacts from his angels:

> Towards him they bend
> With awful reverence prone, and as a god
> Extol him equal to the highest in heaven.[7]

But that it crosses their minds we can infer from the words of Moloch, who seems to have anticipated the bent of Satan's plan and rejected it with contempt:

> My sentence is for open war; of wiles,
> More unexpert, I boast not; them let those
> Contrive who need, or when they need, not now.
> For while they sit contriving, shall the rest,
> Millions that stand in arms, and longing wait
> The signal to ascend, sit lingering here
> Heaven's fugitives, and for their dwelling place
> Accept this dark opprobrious den of shame,
> The prison of his tyranny who reigns
> By our delay?[8]

Hell is the place where you must gouge out your eyes, puncture your ears, and cut off your tongue. Therefore, it is much like our institutions of higher education, as I have

[7] Milton, *Paradise Lost*, 2.477–79.
[8] Ibid., 2.51–60.

noted. Consider how many are the things we must not ask. We must not ask whether certain cultures are superior to others, even though the fact is obvious—and though the very possibility of cultural progress, so central to the progressive vision, is predicated upon it. We must not ask whether certain religions approach nearer to the truth about God and man than others do, even though the humanist confidence in having religiously superseded religion depends upon there being a truth to which we can more nearly approach. We must not ask whether the God who is Love, an identity from Scripture that many an antitheologian is fond of quoting, would so far love the world as to reveal himself to that world he loves, so that men might know the truth about him rather than remain in the gloom and twilight of conjecture.

We must not ask about men and women. We must not pretend to know what the most inattentive observer of human affairs would perceive, which is that in any human situation of any subtlety or complexity, the women will behave like women and the men like men, and that it will be impossible to exchange them one for the other without absurdity. We must not ask about the welfare of children sent off to institutions to spend most of their waking hours before they have given up the rubber nipple. We must not ask about whether our sexual Saturnalia without Saturn, our sad and grimy free-for-all without old-fashioned pagan fertility, our sowing seed into stainless steel tanks or sewers, has made the weakest among us more vulnerable than ever. We must not ask about the black child growing up without a father. We must not ask about the black child not growing up at all but lanced, crushed, and dismembered in the womb.

Higher education of this sort is a black hole where faith, reason, and common observation go to die.

## The Three Stages of the Lie

How do we arrive at the negation? Voegelin describes three stages:

> 1) For the surface act it will be convenient to retain the term Nietzsche used, "deception." But in content this action does not necessarily differ from a wrong judgment arising from another motive than the gnostic. It could also be an "error." It becomes a deception only because of the psychological context.
>
> 2) In the second stage the thinker becomes aware of the untruth of his assertion or speculation, but persists in it in spite of this knowledge. Only because of his awareness of the untruth does the action become a deception. And because of the persistence in the communication of what are recognized to be false arguments, it also becomes an "intellectual swindle."
>
> 3) In the third stage the revolt against God is revealed and recognized to be the motive of the swindle. With the continuation of the intellectual swindle in full knowledge of the motive of revolt the deception further becomes "demonic mendacity."[9]

Voegelin is thinking here of Marx, particularly, but the analysis of the phenomenon admits of far wider application. Again, we should be suspicious whenever we find an obvious question that must not be asked. Not questions that are difficult to answer—there will always be those, and that a system of thought invites questions that the system as yet cannot answer is no proof of its being false. We are looking here for a *willed negation*. We are not concerned with an incomplete grasp of reality. We are concerned with a deliberate embrace of the unreal.

[9] Voegelin, *Science, Politics and Gnosticism*, pp. 25–26.

So then, here we go. You cannot say with one breath that there are no differences between men and women, and then say with the next breath that a man can be a woman in a man's body, or vice versa. If you persist in saying so, you are being more than a poor reasoner. You are a swindler, and you know it. You cannot say that you endorse socialism because you are concerned for the welfare of the poor, while the record of socialist experimentation has been disastrous for the poor. You can bring forth all the tricks of the mountebank to finesse that record, but you are a mountebank nonetheless. The great promoters of nationalized medicine are not unaware that it requires rationing, and the abandoning of the elderly to their diseases, even when the diseases still admit of a cure. They are aware of it, but they may not betray their awareness. They are swindlers.

The gay man knows very well that his sexual life is not in the least like that of an ordinary man, and many will say so openly. But he predicates his claim for a right to "marriage" on indifference: we are to pretend that the lives are the same. It is an intellectual confidence game. The ultimate target of the revolt is the very order of the world as given to us, to conform our passions to that order; the ultimate target is the Creator.

There is a child on the table in the operating room. He is mangled and bloody, but he is alive. He is therefore a citizen of his country, entitled to all the civil rights to which the doctor, the nurse, and his mother are entitled. That is the law of the land, or it used to be.

There is a child in the womb of his mother. He is neither mangled nor bloody, and he is most certainly alive. He has been declared, however, to be a noncitizen until he is born. Before then, he is at the mercy of his mother, who may choose to hire a doctor to kill him, in order ostensibly to safeguard her life, to which in only the rarest of cases does he pose a threat, or to safeguard her "health", which means, as the courts have interpreted it, her psychological view of herself and her life. That is to say, his continued existence poses a threat to her will to interpret her life as she sees fit. He is too real to be permitted to live.

The three stages of the lie are evident in the progress of the public arguments for the abortion license, and the existential arguments in the case of each individual. Publicly, proponents for abortion made a variety of claims that were simply false. They invented statistics with wild abandon. They said that hundreds of thousands of American women, even millions, had died from illegal abortions. The real total was hundreds, over the course of decades. They implied that illegal abortions were self-inflicted and dangerous. But most illegal abortions, by far, were performed by doctors or nurses, who had access to antiseptics and antibiotics. Bernard Nathanson, at one time the head of the National Abortion Rights Action League, admitted later that the information they fed to politicians was fabricated, whole cloth.

It was one thing to exaggerate or to lie, for the nonce. To persist in it, and to allow what you know to have been false to be repeated, and magnified, gossip style, was an intellectual swindle. But after all these years, what can explain the motive? There is perfectly credible evidence that abortion, which involves a radical and unnatural shutdown of the body's cell-transforming process in the midst of a healthy pregnancy, is correlated with breast cancer. The evidence is suppressed or denied. There is perfectly credible evidence that abortion, the killing of one's own child, is correlated with depression, lifelong guilt, and despair. The evidence is suppressed or denied.

Otherwise sane people, and not scientific idiots, say what they know is nonsense, that the fetus is a parasite (parasites are invaders from without, not of the same species as the host, and not the natural and healthy results of reproduction). They will say that the fetus is a clump of cells, like a wart (warts are semipathological growths of skin cells, and not organisms). They will say that the fetus is a part of the mother (parts are parts and not wholes; a finger is a part, but the fetus is a whole). They will say that the fetus is not yet human (of course it is human, as they well know; it is not canine or equine or bovine or anything else but human).

They will say that the decision to abort is one "between the woman and her doctor" (the doctor is for hire, simply, and in any case the radical supporters of abortion want to make it so that doctors cannot refuse to take part). They will say that the woman must be permitted to abort a child that is a result of incest or rape (but incest, if it is not voluntary, is nothing but rape, and the child is an innocent third party, as they well know). They will demand support from the father if the mother keeps the child, but they grant the father no right to interfere in her decision to kill (which is a flagrant contradiction).

They used to say that they wanted abortion to be "safe, legal, and rare", though they dared not explain to us why they wanted it to be rare, and what they were going to do, by way of moral persuasion, to see to it that it was rare. That was a swindle also, because they never raised their voices by one hundredth of a decibel to persuade women to keep the children they had conceived under less-than-ideal circumstances, and because they did nothing to support people who did what they could to ease the mother's burden. But now they have left off saying that they want abortion to be rare. They celebrate it. Female pastors—pastorellas—

in the once-Christian churches of the Left now boast about their abortions and appear to be more deeply devoted to them than to what is left of the Christ their grandfathers and grandmothers once worshiped.

The revolt is against God and the order of the world he has made. Deck it out in a rainbow. The covenant is not between God and man. God looked out upon the world, says the author of Genesis, and saw that the heart of man is wicked from his youth (Gen 8:21). Then came the rain and the flood, and the promise afterward that God made to Noah, that he would never again flood the world, and as a sign of it he set the rainbow in the heavens. Never again, until the end of all, when, as Jesus says, "it will be as in the days of No[ah]" (Lk 17:26).

No, this rainbow is a compact between man and man, against God and creation. The rainbow says that never again will man seek to bring his deeds into harmony with the design of the world he has been given. His world is *his* world: interior, not exterior; self-created, not given; self-determined, not subject to the God who said to the seas, "Hitherto shalt thou come, but no further" (Job 38:11). Hence, we see that Sodom and Moloch go together. Both deny created reality. One gives us sexual intercourse that is not sexual intercourse, and the other begets and consumes children as if they were not children at all. And, to spare the feelings of the gentler sex, it is all set forth in terms of *love*.

"Ye shall be as gods", said the serpent (Gen 3:5).

## Nothing More than Feelings

I do not wish to give the impression here that the lie, as it manifests itself in human action and in demonic rebellion against the Creator, is cold and numb. Milton's Moloch is neither cold nor numb. Robespierre surely whistled while he worked. The crowds cheered lustily while the blade of the National Barber fell. Rousseau, whose philosophy had set the stage for the Barber, was nothing if not a sentimental man.

Never will human beings lie so glibly, or deceive themselves so easily, as when they are talking about their feelings. The reasons are not hard to find. If I say to my wife, "Yes, I painted the picnic table", I know that she can walk out to the backyard and check. But there is no checking someone else's feelings. You can only see them in action, and given the vagaries of feeling and the fact that we sometimes fail to act on them—rather, we sometimes act *against* them—there is no easy way to tell whether and to what extent someone is lying about them. Nor are our own feelings easy to read. I would go so far as to say that for people who do not practice a regular examination of conscience (of one sort or another, such as the Catholic preparation for the sacrament of penance), their feelings can be deeply mysterious to them, depending upon their personalities. Sometimes they can be positively opaque. Many are the parents, for example, who say they feel love for their children, and who have persuaded themselves that they do feel that love, who nevertheless do all in their power to crush them. No doubt the reader has seen a few examples of that.

"Who is it that can tell me who I am?" cries King Lear.[10] That he asks the question at all suggests that he is at least beginning the journey to self-knowledge. There are no traffic jams on that road.

Besides, feelings come and go; they are crucial to the constitution of a virtuous person, as Plato teaches us in the *Phae-*

---

[10] Shakespeare, *King Lear*, 1.4.236.

*drus*, but they cannot be relied upon to lead. They are power-ful assisters of reason—they aspire to reason, you might say, and they are meant to be subject to reason in their character, their direction, and their intensity, but they are not rational in themselves. In man they are stirred or shaken not only by tsunamis but by perfect trifles. The Cardinals win, and I can hear birdsong in a driving rain. I get stuck for a bad lunch at a high price, and I'm kicking the dog when I get home. Our emotions also remain quite unruffled when we know we *should* be feeling something. Jonathan Swift has the true feelings of his own friends pegged, when he writes *Verses on the Death of Dr. Swift*—imagining their reactions after he dies. His female friends (of whom he had many, for Swift was an excellent dinner companion, and with women he was quite a sociable bear) intersperse their expressions of dismay with chat during a game of loo:

> My female friends, whose tender hearts
> Have better learned to act their parts,
> Receive the news in doleful dumps:
> "The Dean is dead: (and what is trumps?)"[11]

It is a feature of the vacuity of our times that even people who call themselves religious will say that their religion is a matter of feeling rather than truth. What happens, then, when talk about feelings predominates in popular piety and the liturgy?

1. We get a version of the Shaker movement—a gnostic confidence that we have entered a New Age, to be led by the Spirit of God, whatever that may be, and wherever the Spirit should take us. I note that said Spirit usually takes us just where the raving of the contemporary already is, and that

---

[11] Jonathan Swift, *Verses on the Death of Dr. Swift*, lines 227–30.

such New Ages rise and fall in the history of the Church with sinusoidal predictability, rather like little Ice Ages or the plague, producing no good art, no profound thought, and no enduring social institutions.

Here I quote Ronald Knox, in *Enthusiasm* (1950), describing the theological vacuity of the Shakers and what happened when an enthusiastic woman came into the community:

> Such a *tabula rasa* as this exactly suited the temperament of a convert who joined them in 1758, Ann Lee. It does not appear that she was a woman of any great spiritual originality. You might have traced in her the influence of Antoinette Bourignon [a perfect lady-tyrant, Catholic heretic, and self-styled visionary, 1616–1680], but that the negative theology of each (both denied the Trinity, the Atonement, and the doctrine of grace) was what you would have expected of a rather stupid woman trying to reinterpret Christian dogma. The conviction that she was a new, female Messiah was more unexpected; yet even here an exactly similar claim was made by another Quakeress, Jemima Wilkinson, in 1786.[12]

Knox is devastating in his swift dismissal of the claims. All he needs to do is to point to some obvious and embarrassing reality: "So disconnected, so departmentalized was the America of those days that it was possible for two female Messiahs, each with her own following, to be accommodated in New York State without either (it seems) having ever heard of the other."

2. People lose the sense of a sharp difference between that talk about feelings and the secrets of the heart, that only God knows. They believe the lies they tell themselves. The Pharisee who made his "confession" at the Temple, while the

[12] Ronald Knox, *Enthusiasm* (New York: Oxford University Press, 1950), p. 559.

publican languished in the back, no doubt felt quite elated by the contrast. He did not know the pride of his own heart. He did not understand his dire need for conversion. It may be the same with us when we sing hymns that *declare* we are happy rather than giving us theological and historical *cause* to be happy. The difference is between a hymn of joy because the Lord is risen, and a hymn *about* our supposed joy, because, don't you know, something important happened two thousand years ago, and I might tell you about it after I get done singing about how joyful I am. Or perhaps nothing important happened two thousand years ago, but it is pretty to think that it did.

3. People are compelled to raise to a liturgical act the necessary hypocrisy of small talk about feelings. Even the innocent hymn centered upon My Feelings can at best be an occasional, extraliturgical outburst: Granny Clampett, stomping left and right and a-singing, "I've got that joy, joy, joy, joy down in my heart!" But if everybody must sing "I am happy, oh so happy", then that will turn most of the congregation into liars—scoff-graces, if I may coin the term. The plain fact is that at any moment in a church, most of the people are *not* especially happy. They may be moderately contented, and that may or may not be a good thing, depending on what they are contented about. Some may be suffering, and that may be a wellspring of devotion for them, if they are suffering with Christ; but some may be suffering the lacerations of their sins. Others may be trekking through the dry land, the waste regions without water. Mother Teresa experienced this; and Saint Thérèse of the Child Jesus, racked with agony as she lay dying of consumption, knew the terrors of feeling utterly abandoned. Christians have cause to be joyful and should sing of that cause: I am certain that Saint John of the Cross, even undergoing the dark night of the soul, sang

exuberantly of the Resurrection of Christ. But the truest feelings are deep and powerful things, of which we know little enough, and about which we should not speak without trepidation.

4. Wary strangers who enter the church are liable to see, instead of devotions that might stir deep feeling, the putting on of an act, a profession of deep feeling. There are two possibilities that enter his mind, neither of them good. The first is that the people are deceiving others or themselves; they do not really feel what they profess. So he leaves, half-disappointed, half-pleased that he can look with some contempt upon people that he would prefer not to have anything to do with. The other possibility is that their professions of feeling seem genuine. But he himself has no such feeling. He can hardly imagine having it. The social critic Erik von Kuehnelt-Leddihn, in *The Timeless Christian* (1969), notes shrewdly that as people differ in their physical prowess, intelligence, originality, and temperament, so too they differ in their capacity for the "spiritual" response, for mystic ravishment, or for devotion broadly conceived. People of only modest spiritual affect learn that church is not for them, in the same way that most lefties learn that golf courses are not for them, or most men learn that quilting is not for them. Reality is for everyone; this or that sentiment, not so.

5. Worst of all, the sentimentality obstructs genuine feeling. Talk long enough and sincerely enough about feelings that you do not feel, and eventually you will cease to be able to feel deeply, whether or not you might have had the words to express the deep feelings. That is because, as a matter of social intercourse again, we place a censor upon the feelings we admit or profess. We know we are *supposed* to feel sad when we hear that an acquaintance has died. We say we feel

sad. We may have to say it, as Dr. Johnson suggested to Boswell; it is a way of speaking in society. But if we dress that supposed sadness up in finery and parade it all the time, if we breathe a false life into the nonfeeling, then we may no longer be fit to distinguish the genuine from the false.

Take, for example, these excerpts from a couple of famous hymns. One is a hymn that expresses a deep feeling —a gentle love but a love that is occasioned by a specific cause. The verses are pregnant with powerful scriptural and theological allusions. "Tarry with us, Lord", said the disciples as they came to the inn outside of Emmaus. "Can God spread a table in the wilderness?" said the children of Israel in their disbelief. "He broke the bread", says the apostle, recounting the moment when Jesus instituted the sacrament of the altar. These allusions, to real events, things that actually happened, lift the feeling from the personal and adventitious to the universal:

> Be known to us in breaking bread,
> But do not then depart:
> Savior, abide with us and spread
> Thy table in our heart.[13]

Then this, a model for the contemporary hymn in praise of our feelings of praise:

> And he walks with me and he talks with me,
> And he tells me I am his own.

Oh, he does, does he? You are one of those rarest of mystics, then? If you were, and you did feel such ravishment of

[13] "Be Known to Us in Breaking Bread," written by James Montgomery, 1825. David Eicher, ed., Glory to God: The Presbyterian Hymnal (Louisville, Ky.: Presbyterian Publishing Corp., 2013).

love, would you sing about it so blithely? Not so did Isaiah:
"Woe is me! for I am undone; because I am a man of unclean lips, and I dwell in the midst of a people of unclean
lips: for mine eyes have seen the King, the LORD of hosts"
(Is 6:5).

## Cosmological Constants

Even the sentiments of the sentimentalist are not always
nice. And in our time the atheist may be the most sentimental soul of all. Let us be careful as always to draw distinctions.

Sentimentality in the liturgy, I have suggested, is destructive of genuine feeling. It is also destructive of rational clar-
ity. Here I recall the famous metaphor that Plato employs
in the *Phaedrus*. Man is like a charioteer with two horses,
one of them noble and high-spirited, the other tending to
be fiery and wayward. The charioteer represents the reason
or intellect. The noble horse represents *thymos*: the "spirit"
or "drive", a noble ambition, the heart in us, the chest. The
wayward horse represents the appetite, the belly and those
regions south of the belly. It is a brilliant metaphor, cap-
turing the truth that without the passions we literally get
nowhere. It also distinguishes passion from passion, inas-
much as there is something about the noble horse that is
friendly to reason; in a sense it aspires to reason. It is wrong
to call it simply irrational.

Now, the whole point of building a chariot and harness-
ing horses to it is so that you can go somewhere, which
implies that there is somewhere to go. You do not race in a
circle for the fun of it, or to lose weight. You have an aim.
You long for the divine. You see as the gods see, says Plato's
Socrates to the lad Phaedrus:

Now a god's mind is nourished by intelligence and pure knowledge, as is the mind of any soul that is concerned to take in what is appropriate to it, and so it is delighted at last to be seeing what is real and watching what is true, feeding on all this and feeling wonderful, until the circular motion brings it around to where it started. On the way around it has a view of Justice as it is; it has a view of Self-Control; it has a view of Knowledge—not the knowledge that is close to change, that becomes different as it knows the different things which we consider real down here. No, it is the knowledge of what really is what it is. And when the soul has seen all the things that are as they are and feasted on them, it sinks back inside heaven and goes home. On its arrival, the charioteer stables the horses by the manger, throws in ambrosia, and gives them nectar to drink besides.[14]

Of course, Plato is speaking metaphorically, but we must not insert the evil word "merely" here. A metaphor is of value for the truth it reveals, and there are some truths, the most important for man, that can best be expressed metaphorically, or that must be so expressed if they are to be expressed at all. The soul thirsts for truth. There is its homeland; there is its joy. I do not long for a happy feeling, so that I then can call it truth. I long for the truth, and the truth brings me peace.

But here is what modern man has done, in brief. The thoughts are by no means original to me. You can find them in Alasdair MacIntyre, or in John Paul II, or in Benedict XVI, or in Dostoyevsky:

Reason is shouldered off the chariot. A small subset of reason, an amputated charioteer, is put in reason's place. What

---

[14] Plato, *Phaedrus*, trans. Alexander Nehamas and Paul Woodruff (Indianapolis: Hackett, 1995), p. 33-34.

is now called "reason" can no longer discuss, rationally, the nature of the good or the beautiful. It cannot be applied to things that are most fully real. It can do two things. First, it can spin out sentences of symbolic logic or mathematics. These, despite their complexity, make assertions that are but tautological, without any real connection to the world of stars and mangrove trees and bicycles. Second, it can manipulate matter according to the physical laws it imputes to the world, inferring those laws (as things that happen to "work", rather than as things that really do exist in themselves) from empirical observations and mathematical analysis. Such reason, a sickly thing, can tell you how to build a Gothic cathedral, but it can give you no cause why you should want to do so.

Imagine that a man could still live after his heart had been torn out of him. Such is man after this amputation of reason. All discussion of the good, the beautiful, and the true (except for the sorts of truths mentioned above) is relegated to the status of "feeling", both by those who pursue the hobby of talking about them, and by those who look upon the hobby as quirky at best and pernicious at worst. This is the position of the emotivists; it is the position Lewis inveighed against in *The Abolition of Man* (1943) and *That Hideous Strength* (1945). It is also the default position in practically every school and university in our country. To say, "X is good", by this argument, is to say no more than "Hurrah for X." It is one short step from there to assume that all aesthetic judgments are merely forms of political partisanship, and likewise all moral judgments. To revel in the beauty and truth of the plays of Shakespeare is to be on the wrong side of some divinized "history", because Shakespeare cannot be brought into the progressive fold. It is, the gnostic emotivist asserts, to be evil.

Professors and students must resist this collapse of reason. Most do not resist. It is always easier to follow the madding crowd.

But if all feelings are merely irrational, if there is no sense to be made of training your feelings so that they will obey the intellect, and if there is no aim to the passionate and the intellectual faculties of man beyond the material and utilitarian, then we must accept as a brute given whatever someone happens to feel. If you feel it, it is good for you. The charioteer lets the reins go free, and the good horse, the horse representing the rationality-aspiring passion for beauty, is eliminated entirely, leaving us with nothing but appetite.

And there it is, appetite in the service of an amputated reason, the second-rate faculty of the intellect that may soon discover how to cobble together monsters of animal and human genetics, without questioning why it should be done, or rather insisting that any moral discussion of it is simply a matter of feeling. And all feelings are irrational.

Sentimentality is a very poor horse, if it is a horse at all and not a hobbyhorse. It is at best a false substitute for *thymos*, in that it dampens the desire for the truly great and beautiful. It turns instead to the easy, to pretty trifles, to the frills and lace of an emotional etiquette, rather than to the deep feelings themselves. And that, as I say, leaves us with nothing but the yawning appetite. And appetite is not nice. It often comes with fangs.

But surely scientists are not ridden by the sentimental, or at least not when they are being scientific. Surely their judgments are to be trusted, because they can be tested. Yes and no.

I once gave a talk on Shakespeare and wonder, for the MacLaurin Institute at the University of Minnesota. The thesis of the talk was that in our grade schools and secondary schools we have scorched the fields of the child's imagination, mystifying the self while slandering or stifling three principal objects of wonder: the hero, the beloved, and God. I had been told that there might be a few opponents in the audience. In fact, the first man to speak up objected. "I am a biologist," he said, "and I do not believe in God, yet when I look at the beauty of nature I think I can feel that wonder you are talking about. So, obviously, belief in God is neither here nor there." You can have the feeling without clear grounds for the feeling, and the feeling is what you want, the affective correlative of an experience of the *truth* of something, and of a beauty that is not to be quantified or reduced to material terms. It is as if you were to go to a waterfall just for the feeling of being at a waterfall, and not to admire it for what the waterfall actually is.

Although I had said that God is the source of our wonder, and the guarantor of its truth, I had been careful also to note that there would always be a few souls, though only a few, who could respond fully to the wondrous beauty of nature or of man while denying the ground of that wonder. In any case, I responded by noting that at all costs I wished to affirm that what I was talking about was not a mere sentiment but a reverence for nobility or grandeur that an object does possess. My fear, I said, is that the unbeliever who begins with that reverence will end, by the force of his logic, by consigning it over to irrelevance. Reverence will be a neural tic; it will depend wholly upon the disposition, even the gastric temperament, of the unbelieving beholder.

I am aware that atheistic scientists can be enthralled with the complexity and magnificence of natural phenomena. The late Carl Sagan was such a man. "The Cosmos is all that is or was or ever will be", he declared, like a priest of a new dispensation. "Our feeblest contemplations of the Cosmos stir us—there is a tingling in the spine, a catch in the voice, a faint sensation, as if a distant memory, of falling from a height. We know we are approaching the greatest of mysteries."[15]

Sagan borrowed all of that language from religion and from religious philosophies such as Platonism. The word "cosmos" itself, as he knew, suggested order and beauty, as in the English derivative "cosmetic": as if the universe had decked itself in glory for our beholding. Why too should we "contemplate" the cosmos? That word suggests a temple, the sacred space set apart for worship. Why should we suppose that we are catching a fleeting glimpse of a "distant memory", as if we could be mindful (Latin *memor*) of an experience we cannot locate in the span of our brief lives? Why should it be a mystery at all, let alone "the greatest of mysteries"? Consider: If the material is all there is, why invest it with all this sentimental frippery? No man says, as he scrapes the mud off the bottom of his shoe, "I am approaching the greatest of mysteries." Yet to say, as Sagan was fond of saying, that we are all made of stuff from the stars, is no more than to say that all is mud—if the material alone is what exists. All else is mere pious sentiment.

As Sagan grew older, he also grew sourer and angrier, more and more determined to show not how beautiful nature was but how beautiful it was not, lest the beholder be brought to the threshold of belief. In that sense he was a sentimentalist, as was my interlocutor in Minnesota. Such men want to bask in what they must concede is simply a feeling, pleasant enough but not logically or empirically warranted by the object. Then when the fit strikes them, they

---

[15] Carl Sagan, *Cosmos* (New York: Random House, 1980), p. 4.

cast themselves into the fire of another feeling, a terrible one, also not logically or empirically warranted by the object. How far the pleasant feeling can take you, as you grow old and your bones ache, or cancer ravages your body and you confront the great fact of death, may be shown by my favorite materialist, the ancient poet Lucretius. He too, as logically ruthless as he thought himself, was another sentimentalist, and he too had a keen eye for the glories of the natural world. So his poem *On the Nature of Things* begins with a hymn to Venus, an allegorical representation of the fecundity of nature:

> Mother of Romans, delight of gods and men,
> Sweet Venus, who under the wheeling stars of heaven
> Rouse the ship-shouldering sea and the fruitful earth
> And make them teem—for through you all that breathe
> Are begotten, and rise to see the light of the sun;
> From you, goddess, the winds flee, from you and your
>     coming
> Flee the storms of heaven; for you the artful earth
> Sends up sweet flowers, for you the ocean laughs
> And the calm skies shimmer in a bath of light.[16]

But the sixth and final book of the poem ends with a horrible description of the great plague of Athens in 430 B.C. The dead and dying are everywhere, and there is no remedy, no consolation, no Epicurean calm—only miserable mankind born to die:

> Many lay flat in the street for thirst, lay prostrate
> Before the fountain-statues of Silenus,
> Breath choked by the great desire for that sweet water.

---

[16] Lucretius, *On the Nature of Things*, trans. Anthony M. Esolen (Baltimore: Johns Hopkins University Press, 1995), bk. 1, lines 1–9.

And strewn about in the roads and parks you'd see
Legs and arms, nerveless, attached to half-dead bodies,
Ragged and dirty, clothes caked with excrement,
Dying, with only bare skin left to the bone,
Nearly buried already in pus and sores and filth.
Yes, all those holy temples of the gods—
Death stuffed 'em with corpses, and the shrines of heaven
Were charnel houses, burdened by cadavers,
Places the priests had filled with worshipers.
Now their religion, now the will of the gods
Meant nothing: present pain was conqueror. . . .
                The suddenness and poverty incited
Horrors. On funeral pyres heaped up for others
People would lay their own kin down, and wail,
And set their torches underneath, and sometimes
Brawl and shed blood, rather than leave their dead.[17]

So the poem ends. Me, I prefer not the *sentiment* of won-der, so quick to flee, but the real thing, granted by God and affirmed by the testimony, objective testimony, of those apostles who have made known to us the power and com-ing of our Lord Jesus Christ, who were eyewitnesses of his grandeur.

## *Magical Unicorns*

It is a plain fact that irreligion in our own modern times has been responsible for the deaths of hundreds of millions of people, and for the destruction, in China, the old Soviet Union, Vietnam, North Korea, and elsewhere, of noble cul-tures that were many centuries in the making. Yet the athe-ist persists in casting religion as the great villain in human

[17] Ibid., 6.1263–85.

history, and in accusing his opponents of incoherence, unreason, bad faith, and unreality.

   Nietzsche knew that the West's loss of faith in God was
a cultural calamity. His feeble heirs are not culturally literate enough to judge the matter one way or another. But
they give themselves away by their obsessions with the unreal. They will say that to believe in God is to believe in a
magic unicorn in the sky, or something foolish like that, and
when they are asked to define what they mean by "magic
unicorn", they shrug and ignore the question. They engage
in the fallacy of *petitio principii*, begging the question, when
they throw at believers what a poorly educated and ill-bred
sophomore might say: "If God created all things, then who
created God?" For the very definition of God that the believing Christian employs is that he is uncreated; you cannot
argue against the existence of uncreated Being by demanding to know about its creation. If you say, "The idea of
uncreated Being is incoherent", you must face immediately
your own self-contradiction, since it is you yourself who
have insisted that the universe itself is uncreated.

   If you say that we can explain the existence of *this* universe by positing the existence of an infinity of universes
(the multiverse), in some of which intelligent life never de-
velops so that beings therein can ask whether their universe
is all there is, you have not moved one millimeter toward
explaining why there should be any universe at all, let alone
an infinitude of them, or why they should have these characteristics rather than those. But you have accomplished one
important feat: you have rejected empiricism. You have rejected the notion that we can speak intelligently only about
what we can observe, and measure, and test. For any universe that is not our own must be inaccessible to us, because
otherwise it would be a part of ours.

The multiverse is the thing that really is like a magical unicorn. It is material, it is said to exist though we can have no evidence of it, and it is invoked to explain what otherwise we cannot explain, though, like the supposititious unicorn, it does not actually explain anything. It is also, like the unicorn, a tad ridiculous. We are to believe, if I understand the theory aright, that an alternate universe exists that is in all respects like our own, but in that universe, or in that universe as it has just diverged string-like from this universe, I paused in my typing these words at just this moment in time to scratch my right posterior rather than my left. And that, that was the beginning of the end, that was what, in that unfortunate other world, led to Armageddon.

Yet as I have said, even if we suppose that an infinite number of universes exists, we have not moved any closer to a solution for the question of existence. It is no help to answer why a stone is here, to say that there is also a stone there. It is no help to answer why there is such a man as John, to say that there is such a man as James. The universe might be as small as the head of a pin, and compared against the omnipotence of God, to say that it is even as large as that is to exaggerate infinitely. The universe might be as enormous as ours is, ever expanding so as to be able to fit within its bounds an ever-larger number of pinheads, some of whom may be named Carl or Daniel or Steven or something. The size is of no consequence.

There is more. The materialist bases his philosophy upon an assumption that is not itself warranted by materialism. It is that the material alone exists. And that embroils him in trouble. He cannot explain consciousness, or the content of human thought, or the works of the imagination. For it is a fact that I know things about what I have not seen, nor will I ever see. I know about the difference between one kind of mathematical infinity (the countable) and another kind (the uncountable). I know about the properties of circles, though I have never seen a circle, only rather bad approximations thereof. I can speak intelligently about Hamlet, who is a creation of the imaginative power of Shakespeare. I can think about the nature of thought; I can posit a category called the "immaterial", where numbers are included, and Platonic forms, and all manner of abstractions from the material.

## Fear of False Gods

Recall again the guess of Epicurus, who said that the disk of the sun was about as large as it appears to our eyes. He was also a flat-earther, that old materialist. Those were strange claims to make in those days, since every educated person knew perfectly well that the earth was round (and Eratosthenes would go ahead and calculate its circumference, accurate within 10 percent). But Epicurus wanted to uphold materialism at all costs, and his materialism took the anti-Platonic position that knowledge not only began in the senses (a position with which Thomas Aquinas would agree) but essentially ended there too. Similarly, Epicurus gave all kinds of possible explanations for the movements of the heavenly bodies. It did not matter which one was true, he said, just so long as none of them involved any deity.

Epicurus was a good man, and if we could exchange modern paganism for his, and preach the temperance, honesty, equanimity, and chastity that he preached, I would make that exchange, no question. He wanted to free his fellow men from their inordinate fears of death and of vindictive gods whom they tried to placate but whom they could never love. The Church Father Lactantius actually praises Epicurus for that, because if a putative god is not the Creator, not infinite goodness, not the source of being and light and love, then that impostor had better be dethroned.

Lactantius understood, in a human way, *why* Epicurus believed what he did, and how he arrived at his deistic conclusion that God, though he exists, has nothing to do with the world one way or another:

> For when Epicurus thought that it was inconsistent with God to injure and to inflict harm, which for the most part arises from the affection of anger, he took away from Him beneficence also, since he saw that it followed that if God has anger, He must also have kindness. Therefore, lest he should concede to Him a vice, he deprived Him also of virtue. From this, he says, He is happy and uncorrupted, because He cares about nothing, and neither takes trouble Himself nor occasions it to another. Therefore He is not God, if He is neither moved, which is peculiar to a living being, nor does anything impossible for man, which is peculiar to God, if He has no will at all, no action, in short, no administration, which is worthy of God. And what greater, what more worthy administration can be attributed to God, than the government of the world, and especially of the human race, to which all earthly things are subject?[18]

Epicurus' strategy is therapeutic, in the context of pagans who feel themselves burdened by fear of the capricious Zeus. We can still see that strategy at work among unbelievers, who tend to mistake that same Zeus for God. It does not

[18] Lactantius, *On the Anger of God*, in *Ante-Nicene Fathers*, ed. Alexander Roberts et al., vol. 7, trans. William Fletcher (Buffalo, N.Y.: Christian Literature Publishing Co., 1886), chap. 4.

matter what explanation we give, so long as no deity is involved. They will cast this strategy as a manful determination to see the truth at all costs, and they accuse believers of simply inserting the answer "God" whenever we encounter a gap in our knowledge of material things. They will not address what the believers—not the sentimentalists—mean by God, because in that case they cannot confuse him either with Mr. Zeus or with a lump of spiritual solder to plug up a hole in a pipe.

I do not mean to say that such flailing explanations are always incorrect; and I do not mean to say either that people who do believe in God never engage in their version of it. I am noting a phenomenon.

The Soviets for a long time derided the notion that the universe had a beginning in time; the regnant materialist cosmology was that of a steady-state universe, with particles instantaneously appearing—*plink!*—out of the void. Napoleon's favorite mathematician, Laplace, once said that if he knew the position of every particle in the universe, he could, theoretically anyway, write the future with absolute certainty. That determinism has been exploded by Heisenberg. Ernst Mach, a materialist and positivist, argued that mathematical objects were only inventions of the human mind, and that all mathematical truths could be assembled from a few basic axioms. Bertrand Russell followed him in the enterprise of attempting to show how this could be so. But Kurt Gödel came along and proved, by mathematical means, that it was not so. He did not mean, as is sometimes supposed, that there are certain axioms that must be taken as given, not proved. Mach and Russell had conceded as much. He meant that in any system with at least the complexity of arithmetic (which is not terribly complex), there will exist nonaxiomatic statements well defined by the system that will be true but that the system will not be able to prove as true. This powerful result—that the truth of mathematics is not limited to the human mind or even to a prospective human mind, since we now know for certain that true statements in these systems exist that the systems cannot demonstrate—seemed to Gödel to be a key plank in proving the existence of God. And in fact, Gödel, a devout Lutheran, adapted his mathematical insights to a new version of the famous argument by Saint Anselm.

My experience with atheists suggests that they simply do not know about Gödel's proof or Anselm's, or the subtlety of the thought of Thomas Aquinas, or the thousand ways in which the Old Testament is nothing like the theogonies and the mythologies of other peoples, or the thousand thousand ways in which Jesus, in the New Testament, is not like any human character either in history or in works of the imagination. They do not know, and they do not want to know. They are ill taught, but then, they insist on remaining so.

Why is this so? Materialism is really untenable; it can be attacked from the vantage of moral imperatives, or Platonism, or mathematics, or cosmology, or metaphysics. What interests me is the motive behind it. It is one thing, because of loss of faith or hope, to fall back upon materialism; I can understand that. I can also understand Epicurus' desire to free men's hearts from their allegiance to such as Zeus and Apollo (and worse). I cannot understand what would make somebody today *want* to believe that materialism is true, which in our country means, for all practical purposes, *wanting* to believe that the man on the cross was wrong, that there is no Father, no ultimate Love, no abiding meaning to what we do, only a grave and dust and oblivion.

Fear of false gods may move those who do not know the true God. But what about fear of the true God?

"But which one is the true God?" asks the atheist, thinking to have scored a point. "You are an atheist with regard to every god but your own. I only increase the number by one." That is a bad argument, because in fact I am not an atheist with regard to every god but God; I believe that men have come to wrong conclusions about God and that they have, in addition, allowed their imaginations to run away with them. I do not believe in Mr. Apollo, but I do believe that the Greeks, in their imaginary Mr. Apollo, though they were not conscious of it, were attempting to express something real about the glory and the beauty of God.

The next dodge is to take the deist position and say that if there is a God, he certainly cannot be a personal God. He is the do-nothing deity of Spinoza, or an indifferent kick-starter of the universe; the Prime Mover that was the object of Aristotle's contemplation; the deity that the reverent Einstein said would not play dice with the universe.

It will not do. The position is born of pride, or a false humility. It is as if we were too tiny and insignificant for God to care about—God apparently being burdened with care for big things like galaxies and quasars, sweating at the controls, and never getting around to reading the messages sent up to him by pneumatic prayer tubes from below. That is foolish. But deism also gives us a leg up on God, and it allows us to look down upon lesser souls who we believe are so foolish as to petition the Non-Almighty Almighty. Ordinary people may pray. We are too smart for that. We despair.

We should consider this business of personhood first.

I am looking at my dog, Jasper. He is a Japanese Chin and Chihuahua mix, looking more like a small spaniel than anything else. He was once a dog in training, learning how to live with human beings, reacting in the proper dogly manner when he was asked, "Do you want to go outside?" or "Do you want some food?" He responds to more than eighty commands, and he is the only dog I have ever owned from whom I must sometimes conceal information. If I say, "Your friends are coming today", he will be nervous until the doorbell rings.

Jasper is, according to a former colleague of mine in biology, a machine; but that is bad biology, bad linguistics, and bad metaphysics. A machine is typically an imitation animal, whose parts work according to some concatenated and therefore strictly artificial order. It is organized, so to speak, but it is not an organism. A single bacterium possesses a complexity, an integrated unity among its parts, and an ability to interact with its environment, that makes the computer I am typing on seem rather like a rock sitting inert in a field. The bacterium is fully bacterial in every one of its mutually interacting features. The rock *has* being, but the bacterium *is* a being, a living thing. So much the more Jasper, who at the moment is chewing happily upon a piece of rawhide.

What Jasper is not—and the car is not, and the computer is not, and the rock in the field is not—is a person. Dietrich von Hildebrand once said that after the division between being and nonbeing, the greatest divide in being was not between living and nonliving being but between personal and impersonal being. What separates my dog from the rock in the field is not so great as what separates my dog from me. This appears counterintuitive to us, I think, only because we forget how wondrous a thing man is. We have lost our hold on the fullness of reality. Christians are almost the only humanists left—by which I mean the only people who would understand what moved Michelangelo to paint *The Creation of Adam*, or what moved the blind Milton to lead up in poetic climax to the single sight he missed the most, the "human face divine".[19] We see that the dog has eyes and ears and nose and mouth, and we have eyes and ears and nose and mouth; we walk, the dog walks; we eat, the dog eats. So we draw the conclusion that we are like the dog, and, as far as the likeness goes, we are right; but we forget that at the same time we are like the source and end of personhood, God—and that likeness penetrates to the core of our being.

For it is a great mystery, this of personhood. Imagine the universe without a single person to observe it and to revel in its beauty. What a gray and futile thing it is! But with the creation of a person, something enters the universe that in a real sense is greater than the universe. For the universe cannot understand itself. It cannot love itself. It cannot imagine itself as other than it is. It cannot encounter anything. It exists, but it cannot say, "I exist", much less "You exist", and, more marvelous still, "How wonderful it is that you exist!" My dog Jasper likes me. He capers and jumps up and down when I come home from work. But he does not pause before the mystery of me. He does not reflect upon me. He does not ask, "What is it like to be my master?" He looks into my eyes when I scratch him behind the ears, but he cannot say, "What is good for you will be good for me", or "Because I love you, I give myself wholly to you."

There are no ordinary people, said C. S. Lewis. When you meet a person, you are encountering someone "a little lower than the angels" (Ps 8:5; Heb 2:7), someone not only capable of the cardinal virtues that make for a half-decent

---

[19] Milton, *Paradise Lost*, 3.44.

city but, by the grace of God, capable of faith, hope, and charity. My dog Jasper is close to God in this sense: he does what a dog ought to do. But he cannot worship. He cannot pray. He cannot respond to God in love. When I say, "I see the dog", I am affirming the startling existence of someone, myself; and it may be that my affirmation of my own existence, as a person, depends upon my affirmation of the Person who made the world wherein my personhood has come into being.

For it makes no sense to notice a power in me that would be lacking in God. I can say, "I", and I intend by that pronoun a being that can grasp time itself, and that perdures through time and can step to the side of time; I can say, "Perhaps I will do such and such", or, "If only I had done thus and so." That is a dynamism, not a limitation. I can love, and love, as Plato saw, is not simply a result of my penury, my lack of something I desire; it is the flowing forth of the self toward the beloved, and in God it brings the beloved itself into being. It is a contradiction to see love as a power and then to deny that God loves. If I am not only an object but a subject, then so much the more must God be a subject: God is pure act, God knows, God loves. So superabundant is he in personhood, he is, as he has revealed to us, a communion of Persons, Father, Son, and Holy Spirit.

## Thou Art Not

Now to bind all these assertions of mine together.

Suppose two things. Grant that when God spoke to Moses from the burning bush, and gave his name as the name beyond naming, "I AM", he revealed himself to be not a supreme being merely, the greatest in a series, but to be

Being itself, the source of all being. Grant also that man, alone among any creatures that we know of in this universe, is like the angels, made in the image and likeness of God.

If we lose hold of these truths, what happens? What happens when we say to God, explicitly or implicitly by our actions, "Thou art not"?

Initially, man pretends to a surer hold upon reality than he had before, just because he limits himself to those things he can quantify. "Facts, facts, facts!" cries that essential utilitarian and empiricist, Thomas Gradgrind. "Teach these children nothing but facts!" The physical sciences appear to continue unharmed, but it is as if there were a parasite gnawing at their vitals, unseen, or an acid working silently at the core. For the materialist as such can no longer speak sensibly of unitary beings. There is only matter, and matter will not suffice to explain why we speak as if it were the same tree in the yard as yesterday, when its matter is in constant flux. I scratch my arm and send to perdition some thousands of cells. I am not the man I used to be. What gives me any warrant to use the personal pronoun at all? Not my memory, which is also in flux, and which is often mistaken.

What about the current organic structure into which my matter is organized? That too changes, and indeed it is impossible, on those grounds, to say of the unborn child in the womb that it is the same being as the child, or that the child before puberty is the same as the child afterward, or that the man in the process of dying is the same as the man before he was afflicted with the disease that will end him.

We can suppose, then, that the worst offenses against the personhood of human beings and against the integrity and beauty of creatures will come in the wake of the denial of ultimate reality. There is no reason, founded in materialism, for me to distinguish rubbing out a man from rubbing out the mud at the bottom of my shoe, because materialism is just a philosophy of mud. The mud may glisten in the sun. The mud may be a composite of silicon and carbon, hydrogen and nitrogen, titanium and aluminum and an array of other elements. Wonderful it is, but in the end it is mud. Carl Sagan may say that we are all made of stardust, but that too is just mud, star mud.

What we do with mud is also of no great moral import. Clump it into bricks and let them dry in the sun; why not? All the inhuman collectives of the twentieth century have been predicated upon man as mud. You can build many a pyramid from such. Consider the chasm in being that divides the collective from the community. Persons in the collective are submerged under numbers, nameless and faceless. If we regard the mass phenomena, we can see that the submergence of the person occurs in capitalist as well as in socialist countries, such as they now are. The great virtue that is both the foundation and the aim of the polis, according to Aristotle, is friendship. That can be conceived only among persons. The vice of the collective, by contrast, is either apathy or enmity: apathy, because the person, with a name and a face, with thoughts that reach far into the past and that long for the everlasting, is reduced to a thing, a counter, a clump of mud; enmity, because what is left of our God-endowed particular humanity rises up in resentment against the offense.

You can also treat your own self as mud. You are not made in the image of God. Therefore, you assume the prerogative of a god and pretend to make yourself according to your own imagination. You do not, for example, take your sex as a given, and as a beautiful thing to which you must submit in wonder and gratitude. You take it as you would

170 SEX AND THE UNREAL CITY

take a heap of mud, to do with as you please—to destroy, to rearrange, to corrupt, to fashion into an idol.

Talk of morality is then sheer sentimentality. So is talk about rights. A right implies a duty: an obligation to honor something that may not profit me at all. The atheist Steven Pinker has sneered at the notion of "dignity", which cannot apply to mud. The word suggests a real character that is *dignus*, worthy of honor and reverence. If you are not worthy of honor and reverence, what "rights" can you reasonably claim? You cannot rely upon civil rights, which then will be based upon nothing but civil consensus, and the consensus can change. Besides, whenever anyone argues that a law is unjust, or that we should abandon our consensus regarding a certain behavior considered immoral, he implies that good and evil actually exist; but he has no way to justify how he identifies them, unless he appeals to an unchanging standard, however it may be imperfectly understood or realized in any one society. Without that hold upon us, without a sense of moral reality that binds us regardless of what we please, we must revert to power, whether with the noise of political action or with fists and guns.

Some few people, most of them male, will draw the correct conclusion, which is pure nihilism. Good and evil do not form societies, but societies form what is supposed to be "good" and "evil". Then there is no good or evil. Then there is nothing for it, as Flannery O'Connor's notorious Misfit says, but to kill and rape and steal and do meanness to others, getting some fun out of life. Most people—and females especially will favor this conclusion—will coat their nihilism with a gloss of sweet sentimentality, and say that everybody has his or her own view of what is good, and that everybody just ought to be nice to everybody else. Niceness apparently includes all manner of sexual perversion and the snuffing out of unborn children. Humanitarianism, says

Walker Percy, leads to the gas chamber. Relativism is nihilism for girls. The relativist lioness extends her pinky-
claw while she rips out your guts. It doesn't mean she isn't
a nice creature.

## Beauty Is Not

If man is not man but mud, and if he is not oriented toward
the God in whose image he has been made, then he must lose
his sense of the three transcendentals: the good, the true,
and the beautiful. Goodness collapses into utility, truth is
narrowed down to what is quantifiable, and beauty is either nothing at all—as "Gaius" and "Titius" say, in Lewis'
*Abolition of Man*—or pretends to take up residence in the
hideous, the offensive, the dark, the miserable. We Americans are the wealthiest people ever to walk the earth. But our
public buildings are drab or hideous, or lamely and unim-
pressively derivative of architectural styles that we did not invent and could not now invent. Medieval man built Chartres
Cathedral. We build shopping malls and football stadiums.
Whole genres of art have shriveled like a spider. Where is
the tradition of modern portraiture? There is none. Where
is the modern dramatic monologue in verse? No one writes
such. Where is the modern cantata? The modern oratorio?
The modern epic?

It is a moonscape. "I consider that the way of life in ur-
banised, rich countries, as it exists today, and as it is likely
to go on developing," wrote Malcolm Muggeridge, many
years before his full conversion to the Christian faith,

> is probably the most degraded and unillumined ever to
> come to pass on earth. The half-century in which I have
> been consciously alive seems to me to have been quite ex-
> ceptionally destructive, murderous and brutal. More peo-
> ple have been killed and terrorised, more driven from their

Women

homes and native places; more of the past's heritage has been destroyed, more lies propagated and base persuasion engaged in, with less compensatory achievement in art, literature and imaginative understanding, than in any comparable period of history.[20]

When man stands humble and naked before the God who is, the encounter stretches him from nothingness to infinity. So cries the poet Herbert in "The Temper (I)":

> O rack me not to such a vast extent;
>> Those distances belong to thee:
>> The world's too little for thy tent,
>>> A grave too big for me.[21]

But that stretching, that building up of a human soul out of nothing, that redemption from the antibeing that is sin, is a work of God that brings forth beauty within the soul:

> Yet take thy way; for sure thy way is best:
>> Stretch or contract me thy poor debtor:
>> This is but tuning of my breast,
>>> To make the music better.[22]

Which beauty brings forth beauty from the human artist, as when Herbert imagines setting forth on Christmas Day to find a sun, or a Son, who will raise up his music to heights that otherwise he could never attain:

> I will go searching, till I find a Sun
>> Shall stay, till we have done;
> A willing shiner, that shall shine as gladly
>> As frost-nipt suns look sadly.

[20] Malcolm Muggeridge, *Jesus Rediscovered* (Garden City, N.Y.: Doubleday, 1969), 119.

[21] George Herbert, "The Temper (I)", lines 9–12.

[22] Ibid., lines 21–24.

Then we will sing, and shine all our own day,
        And one another pay:
His beams shall cheer my breast, and both so twine,
Till even his beams sing, and my music shine.[23]

Man made in God's image and therefore longing, as the psalmist says, "to behold the beauty of the LORD, and to enquire in his temple" (Ps 27:4), is like Michelangelo's Adam, extending a hand toward his Creator, to receive the breath of life from him. His spirit is flung forth into Being, and he accomplishes what would otherwise be, if not technically impossible for him, inconceivable. Bach without the God to whom he prayed and from whom he took inspiration is not Bach; he is a technician on a machine. Michelangelo without the God to whom he prayed and from whom he took inspiration is not Michelangelo; he is a brooding half-autistic man with a chisel and darkness in his heart. Shakespeare without God is his own Timon of Athens, a well-spoken cynic.

And we, without God, are foolish, self-absorbed without much of a self to be absorbed into; and the art we make is also foolish and dreary, sentimental and numb at once. Will art in our time ever be raised from the dead? Not by our unaided and prideful efforts, which have only stifled it all the more. Only God can raise the dead. Our liturgies themselves, insofar as they are ours and not God's, are brightly colored dirges, and the churches where we celebrate, insofar as they are ours and not God's, are but charnel houses, mausoleums.

[23] George Herbert, "Christmas", lines 27–34.

## Crumbling into Nothing

At this point we must face the ultimate questions. The lie—
the evasion—will not do. God either exists, or he does not.
If he exists, he has either revealed himself fully in Christ,
or he has not. These are questions as to fact. If God exists,
and if Christ is the coeternal Son of the Father in whom
we live and move and have our being, then consequences
must follow. We can no longer lie to ourselves. We cannot
pretend that good and evil hang upon our happenstance def-
initions. Poison works no matter what we may pretend it
is. Good and nourishing food builds us up, no matter what
somebody else may say about it. When we say that a certain
act is evil, we are affirming a fact, and we affirm that consequences must follow from it, as inevitably as they follow
from any other reality. We do not claim that some supposititious deity may punish it in an afterlife. We claim that it is
its own punishment, now, because God has not made us for
untruth, and if we embrace untruth, we hug nothingness,
and we begin to evacuate our souls, till in the end all that
remains is a wraith where a fully realized soul should have
been, a shell of humanity.

Every time, then, we encounter an untruth about man,
or every time we meet people who behave as if the true
worship of God were wholly or principally in our determination rather than being bestowed upon us by God as a gift,
we look upon a person or an institution set on the brink
of a chasm, blithely unaware of it, and apt to fall into the
nothingness with the next false step. No one who sees the
brink and the certain destruction that it threatens can say,
"It does not matter which next step we take." But people
around us do say that, all the time. I suggest here that that
is not because they feel the solid earth under their feet—

the good, solid, dependable foundation of this God-created reality. It is because they no longer feel anything under their feet. For them the world itself has been thinned out into a dream, a supposition, a set of opinions. "I am my own light", says the liar, and he shuts his eyes, and dances toward what is not there.

# 5

# Return to Reality

I believe in God,
the Father almighty,
Creator of heaven and earth,
and in Jesus Christ, his only Son, our Lord,
who was conceived by the Holy Spirit,
born of the Virgin Mary,
suffered under Pontius Pilate,
was crucified, died and was buried;
he descended into hell;
on the third day he rose again from the dead;
he ascended into heaven,
and is seated at the right hand of the God the Father
    almighty;
from there he will come to judge the living and the dead.
I believe in the Holy Spirit,
the holy catholic Church,
the communion of saints,
the forgiveness of sins,
the resurrection of the body,
and life everlasting. Amen.[1]

---

[1] Apostles' Creed, in "Prayers of the Rosary", United States Conference of Catholic Bishops, last accessed March 11, 2020, http://www.usccb.org/prayer-and-worship/prayers-and-devotions/rosaries/prayers-of-the-rosary.cfm.

The cynic scoffs. "You talk of reality, and in one breath you give us nothing but your opinion about a myth."

No myth, but fact. The truth to which whatever is true in human myths points; the truth whereof those myths, as Tolkien said, were "good dreams". Fact, solid fact.

I affirm here that those words above hold the key to solving all the intellectual, moral, social, and spiritual dilemmas that we find otherwise insoluble. They do not and they cannot give us an experience of the fullness of reality, because that can be promised to us only by God. It is not available to us in this world, frail and dim and sinful as we are. They do give us the fullest experience of reality that we can have; they clear away the unreality; they bring together realities that might seem opposed to one another; they provide a real foundation for society, for intellectual inquiry, for art, and for that love that soars beyond the best of the pagan ideals of friendship. Let me take up the affirmations one by one. All I can give are hints, glimpses of whatever small portion of the truth these affirmations have permitted me to see. Let the reader pray and proceed further than I have gone.

## I Believe in God, the Father Almighty

The world about us cannot rest upon itself, because it is made up of contingent beings, things that need not have been at all, and the characteristics of this world bear no necessity within them. It is absurd to suppose that being can rest upon nonbeing. To say, then, "God exists" is not to plug up a hole in the beings that we perceive but to reason from the manner in which things about us exist, to the necessary existence of Being beyond all contingent characteristics and happenstances. For everything around us is, as

Augustine says, an "is/is not", unnecessary, and tending toward dissolution. Then there must be something that purely *is*. Hence did God reveal to Moses the name that is not a name at all, the name beyond names: "I AM".

In every pagan system I know of, we begin with unformed stuff, and a theogony, that is, a genealogy of the gods. Ouranos begat Cronus, and Cronus begat Zeus. Only in Genesis is there no unformed stuff at the origin of things, but rather God, who in the beginning made the heavens and the earth. The author gives us no genealogy of God or from God. The begats are relegated to man as presented in history: Adam begat Cain and Abel, and so forth, proceeding down to Abraham, "father of many" (Gen 17:5), the progenitor of the children of Israel.

In every pagan system I know of, some god or other will perform some operation upon some preexisting matter and make things from it: the Hebrew word would be *'asa*, translated by the Greeks as *poiein*, "to make". But God created, which is to do more than to make: the Hebrew word, much rarer and predicated only of God, is *vara*. We may infer the difference between these actions by the means God uses to create. There is no instrumentality. He simply speaks: "And God said, Let there be light: and there was light" (Gen 1:3). The Hebrew is stunningly powerful in its terseness and its linguistic identity between what God says and what comes to be: "*W'yomer Elohim, Yehi 'or, w' yehi'or.*" There is no lapse between the speaking and the being. There is not even a linguistic distinction between the speaking and the being: it is *yehi 'or* on both sides. God imparts being to what has no being, because he is Being: the verb he speaks is a form of his own name, that which the faithful Hebrew would not utter. Being is holy.

Why light and not mud? What do we make out of light?

You cannot build a city upon blocks of light. But you can perhaps build a city or a human soul only upon the light, which is truth and goodness and beauty. That it is light and not mud reveals to us that the world is open to the light of the intellect: it is filled with intelligible light. God himself beholds the light and declares it to be good, *ki tov*, as the Hebrew has it, the same words the psalmist uses when he cheers us on to give thanks to the Lord, for he is good: *ki tov*. God makes good things because it is good to exist, and he is both existence and goodness.

Light is the perichoresis, the dancing-among, from existence to goodness to beauty. God himself "only hath immortality, dwelling in the light which no man can approach unto" (1 Tim 6:16), for no man can comprehend God. But he pours forth his light, "for with thee is the fountain of life: in thy light shall we see light" (Ps 36:9). Then we too, by that light, find the goodness and the beauty of being, and we grow in being and in understanding as we draw nearer to the light. Now, this drawing-near is not to be understood abstractly, nor is the giver of light an impersonal force, as Plotinus and the Neoplatonists, so near to the truth, imagined. God is Father—and that is to be taken not as a human metaphor but as a proper name, describing God's relation to all created things. He has not generated them out of his own body, as a mother would; he has begotten them by willing them, by speaking them into being.

The light, then, is personal and demands a personal response. So says the Lord: "He that hath my commandments, and keepeth them, he it is that loveth me: and he that loveth me shall be loved of my Father, and I will love him, and will manifest myself to him" (Jn 14:21). John Keats called this world a "vale of soul-making", and in his Romantic fashion he struck a great part of the truth. It is from the very begin-

ning a world immersed in the personhood of God, to be a
world of persons, loving one another because they respond
in love to the God who made them.

## And in Jesus Christ, His Only Son, Our Lord

People of our time are fond of repeating, without much
understanding, the words of Saint John, that "God is love"
(1 Jn 4:8). They do not repeat the verse that is wonderfully
parallel to it, that "God is light, and in him is no darkness
at all" (1:5). Love is not love without truth, and he who
says he has the truth but does not love is no better than a
liar. But when people say that God is love, they seem to
subordinate God to our desires; God is a yo-yo, falling and
rising in concert with the desires of our wrists. That is not
God but a fiction, just as not one of our desires is pure,
and they all threaten to veer off into unreality, unless God
should be their foundation and their aim.

To say, however, that God *is* love is to say more than that
God loves. For love is essential to God. He does not begin
to love when he begins to create. He is himself love, and so,
though the full truth of it must remain to us as dwelling in
inaccessible light, he is himself a communion of Persons, a
loving society. Let the inimitable Chesterton, from *Orthodoxy*, express the implications:

> If this love of a living complexity be our test, it is certainly
> healthier to have the Trinitarian religion than the Unitar-
> ian. For to us Trinitarians (if I may say it with reverence)
> —to us God Himself is a society. It is indeed a fathomless
> mystery of theology, and even if I were theologian enough
> to deal with it directly, it would not be relevant to do so
> here. Suffice it to say here that this triple enigma is as com-
> forting as wine and open as an English fireside; that this

thing that bewilders the intellect utterly quiets the heart:
but out of the desert, from the dry places and the dreadful
suns, come the cruel children of the lonely God; the real
Unitarians who with scimitar in hand have laid waste the
world. For it is not well for God to be alone.[2]

Unitarians may be liberals and often are, but that is an ac-
cident of Western social history, because nothing in their
theology suggests it. The theology instead would suggest a
pure will, that of the "lonely god of Omar or Mahomet".
We in the West have had the Mohammedanism of ideology
—men like Marx, half-mad, hating everything wrong in the
world and hating man all the more for it, seeking to impose
upon everyone the dictates of their single wills, aflame. But
the Christian who looks with love upon the three-Person
God sees not lonely ideology but love, the giving and receiving of gifts, within the divine life itself. Edward Gib-
bon sneered and said, of the early Christian controversies,
that they were all about a diphthong: whether Christ was
*homo-ousios*, "one in being" with the Father, or merely *ho-
moiousios*, "like unto" the Father. He did not see that the
character of all the world, and of human society itself, rested
upon the distinction. The distance between unity alone and
Trinity is at least as vast as the difference between a lesser
god to whom we cannot appeal and the God who hears our
prayers.

## He Was Made Man

The Incarnation is the central mystery of the Christian faith.
So Dante, at the end of the *Paradiso*, is wholly drawn into di-

[2] G. K. Chesterton, "The Romance of Orthodoxy", in *Orthodoxy* (San
Francisco: Ignatius Press, 1995), p. 142.

vinity not by the mystery that God might create beings that are not God, or even that God is three Persons in one, but by the mystery that God would become man to share man's sorrow and to love man even to the end, to death upon a cross. To grasp even the slenderest of truths about Christ is to touch the key to all human questions, for through him all things were made (Jn 1:3), and "in him was life; and the life was the light of men" (1:4).

What do we mean when we say so? It is not enough to compare Jesus with Buddha the benevolent world-denying mystic, or with Confucius the traditional adviser of gentlemen, or with any wise man like Socrates, who by comparison with Jesus appears to be a mischievous peddler of words. The very act seems not simply impious. It seems unreal. When William Wyler, a Jew, directed the film *Ben-Hur*, he did not show the viewers the face of Jesus, because it struck him that no actor could suffice. Yet Jesus had a human countenance like anyone else: we may, I believe, behold it in photographic negative upon the famous Shroud.

We mean that Jesus, fully human, is fully divine, and became fully human because he was fully divine, that is, filled with love for poor, benighted, sinful, mortal man. Saint Paul:

> Let this mind be in you, which was also in Christ Jesus:
> Who, being in the form of God, thought it not robbery to be equal with God:
> But made himself of no reputation, and took upon him the form of a servant, and was made in the likeness of men:
> And being found in fashion as a man, he humbled himself, and became obedient unto death, even the death of the cross.
> Wherefore God also hath highly exalted him, and given him a name which is above every name:

> That at the name of Jesus every knee should bow, of things
>     in heaven, and things in earth, and things under the earth;
> And that every tongue should confess that Jesus Christ is
>     Lord, to the glory of God the Father. (Phil 2:5–11)

Christ reveals man to himself, said the Council Fathers at Vatican II. Then to be made in the image of God, through Christ, is to be made like the one who gave fully of himself, the eternal submitting to the ravages of time, the selfsame subject to change, the source of life becoming by death the gate of life to men who are born and grow old and die. To imitate Christ is not the same kind of thing as to imitate Buddha, or even one of the Christian saints. It is to join yourself to Christ, who gives us our being by his love. He reveals to us the heart of life, into which it is impossible to penetrate any further, because by definition there can be no further: there can be no fuller self-emptying than that of God, becoming man, and enduring the nothingness of ignominy, shame, and abandonment by his friends and by the very people he came to save. Nothing so conveys the reality of his anguish as does his cry from the cross, in his childhood tongue, Aramaic: "My God, my God, why hast thou forsaken me?" (Mt 27:46). The Father with whom he had so intimate a love, for "the Son can do nothing of himself, but what he seeth the Father do" (Jn 5:19), seemed to him to have withdrawn his presence. By comparison with the death of Jesus, our deaths seem vague and unreal. For our spirits have sojourned in a world of unreality, our world of sin.

Do we suffer? Jesus suffered too, and he suffered what we sinners can never know. He suffered having to peer into man's emptiness. He suffered not only the weight of our sin. He suffered its nothingness. He knew all that will make us angry. But we will never know one part in a thousand of what made him *disappointed*:

Now when he was in Jerusalem at the passover, in the feast day, many believed in his name, when they saw the miracles which he did.

But Jesus did not commit himself unto them, because he knew all men,

And needed not that any should testify of man: for he knew what was in man. (Jn 2:23–25)

To know Jesus is to know the truth about both God and man, and here is a truth we resist, because we are too timid for it. When Jesus said, "Blessed be ye poor: for yours is the kingdom of God" (Lk 6:20), he was not making a promise to be fulfilled in a distant land of the imagination. He was making a claim about reality. He was stating a fact. On the surface it is like what the wise men of the world have said, because they know that too much wealth will cramp us and bind our hearts to vanity. Even the Epicureans knew it. Diogenes the Cynic went so far as to use a barrel for his dwelling. He moved his bowels in the public square. That is not the poverty Jesus has in mind.

The poor are blessed because it is easier for them to break open the shells of their hard hearts. The rich will tend to love riches; it is how many people become rich in the first place, "for where your treasure is, there will your heart be also" (Mt 6:21). Suffering, said Pope John Paul II, is for the unleashing of love. If we were not sinners, it would need not be so. The saints in heaven have no need any longer to suffer for the unleashing of love. We do have that need. Says Herbert:

> A heart alone
> Is such a stone
> As nothing but
> Thy power doth cut.[3]

---

[3] George Herbert, "The Altar", lines 5–8.

And why should we believe that the cracking open of that heart of stone will be done or can be done without a suffering like that of a woman in labor? Or without pain that pierces to the heart?

The pagans at their best might glimpse the truth, vaguely. We might be told the truth a thousand times, and assent to it, and still not really believe it. Hence Truth himself comes to pitch his tent among us, so that what might otherwise remain an abstraction in the mind, a theoretical possibility, is manifest to us in flesh and blood. Jesus is not a theoretical possibility. He was a man "in all points tempted like as we are, yet without sin" (Heb 4:15). Yet there is more. The Incarnation is not merely one way among other possibilities for our redemption. It reveals the heart of love and the reality of Being. The pagans could conceive of Being as self-sufficiency. They could not conceive of it as love. But to be a person at all is to *be for*: goodness is diffusive of itself, say the schoolmen. Goodness is multiplicative. It grows by giving. God would not be God without possessing an infinitude of giving; and this giving and receiving is the inner life of the Trinity. When Jesus says, "Whosoever exalteth himself shall be abased; and he that humbleth himself shall be exalted" (Lk 14:11), he is not making a promise or issuing a threat. He is declaring a law of being itself. Think of how petty appears to us now the self-exaltation of an Augustus Caesar, having himself sculpted as the pious Pontifex Maximus on the altar he commissioned to commemorate himself as the prince of peace. Think of the faded glory of a Tamerlane, a Genghis Khan, a Napoleon. Their glory was ever one part accomplishment and nine parts show. A man might learn political tactics from Augustus. If he said to us, "I want to learn from Augustus what it is to be a human being", we would glance to the telephone and consider calling the men in white coats. No one, not even a scoffing atheist, would have that reaction were we to say, "I want to learn from Jesus."

## In the Flesh

And we return to matter. Christians take matter seriously. It is strange that atheistic scientists, who say on Monday that nothing exists but matter, on Tuesday, embarrassed by the particularity of that same matter, will resolve it into immaterial mathematical laws, going so far as to say not only that matter *obeys* the laws but that matter is *nothing other than* those laws. First we lose the immaterial soul, and then we lose the material body. There is no meaning to that body. So we see the inner connection between materialism and the vagaries of the gnostic. If the body is unreal, why should we not do whatever we please with it, especially in the realm of sex? If there is no soul, how can what we do with the body hurt us, if it does not hurt the body?

"Except I shall see in his hands the print of the nails," said Thomas the stubborn, "and put my finger into the print of the nails, and thrust my hand into his side, I will not believe" (Jn 20:25). I once heard a silly television newsman say, on Easter, that this was the day when Christians celebrate the rising of Jesus' soul to heaven. Any pagan could have done as much for any pagan hero. It would have been like celebrating the apotheosis of Julius Caesar. Thomas wanted no such vagary. He wanted to see the body, to touch it, to feel in its undeniable particularity the *person of Jesus*, body and soul. Jesus was not a corpse, not a ghost, and not, though I hear it from ignorant scoffers, a "zombie". He was Jesus, raised from the dead, in the flesh, in the body glorified, for "it is sown a natural body; it is raised a spiritual body" (1 Cor 15:44). They who know their physics may deny it, but they of all people may not snicker, for they know too much mathematics for that, and too much about how nearly does matter without organization flicker on the brink of nonexistence. They who can imagine another universe besides this one, the only one for which they have any evidence, dare not then declare that matter can assume no other forms but those we see, and obey no other laws but those we infer.

But he was raised in the flesh, as the master Caravaggio shows in his painting of doubting Thomas, as Jesus, with infinite patience, guides the apostle's finger into his pierced side. Caravaggio declares, "This is real flesh, disturbingly real." We should like our Savior to be spiritual, conveniently so. I can sin with all the freer abandon so long as I remain "spiritual".

Yet when I lie dying, what will that spirituality be to me, if it is divorced from the body and all that I have experienced in the body? To say that Jesus dwelled among us is not to say that he went slumming for a time. It is also to reaffirm the Creator's declaration in the beginning: "And God saw every thing that he had made, and, behold, it was very good" (Gen 1:31). God dwells in his fullness in the tiniest particle of existence. What is in "the smallest of all seeds" (Mt 13:32)? Chesterton tells us:

> God Almighty, and with Him,
> Cherubim and seraphim,
> Filling all eternity:
> Adonai Elohim.[4]

The Resurrection of Christ in the flesh is a promise. Nothing of the goodness of this life will be lost. We will be-

---

[4] G. K. Chesterton, "The Holy of Holies", lines 13–16.

hold the full truth whereof our artistic flights were like the groping of the half blind, for now "we see through a glass, darkly" (1 Cor 13:12). We will see the faces of loved ones, who derive their personhood from God, whose face we have sought. There will be "a new heaven and a new earth" (Rev 21:1). The dog who lies sleeping now at my feet as I write these words, my dog Jasper whose terminus on this earth draws nearer so much more quickly than does mine —what of him? It has not been revealed, but this we know: no good seed falls to the rich earth without fruit. And God, who gives us what we have never dreamed of, may well give us our good dreams too.

Is there more? Far more, and always more. For love does not know of less. When God revealed himself to Moses, as I have said, he identified himself as Being: I AM. But then, as it were, he incarnated himself in history: "Thus shalt thou say unto the children of Israel, the LORD God of your fathers, the God of Abraham, the God of Isaac, and the God of Jacob, hath sent me unto you" (Ex 3:15). The ancient pagans had a faint sight of the God whose essence it is *to be*. The modern progressive, in a cultural swoon, declines from that God and falls in worship of the process of history, which is supposed to lead us to everything sweet and good, such as was made manifest in the Soviet Union and Maoist China and the Third Reich, and is made manifest now in the exhaustion of Europe, whose sacred termini are abortion and euthanasia. But the God of history, that personal God, chooses a certain people to bear witness to him, these and no other, and not for their merits; and he chooses each man alive for this task, for this family, for this city, for this school, for this poor suffering fellow human being, for this little child in the womb, for this sweet plot of land, for this small church, for this embodiment of holiness, for glory.

## The Spirit and the Church

One of the "conservative" unrealities of our time is a belief in the primacy of the individual.

I like to point out to my students that the main thing that marks out Mr. Cyclops as a barbarian is not that he possesses a single eye in the middle of his forehead. No doubt Miss Cyclops finds it handsome and bats her eyelash at him when they flirt. It is that the Cyclops and his fellows never come together in assembly. Each one minds his flocks and his cave, and every family ignores its neighbors. If it were not for the ocular peculiarity, I would think that my nation had been invaded by the Cyclopean. If you go to an airport you will notice that no one takes notice of anyone else. Everyone has his eye fixed on a screen.

That is not much of a human life. Yet it is the life to which we are condemned if we take the view that the individual, an isolated cell of will, is the fundamental unit of human society. It cannot be, because *that is not what man is.* Aristotle said so, when he declared that man by nature is a political animal, meaning that man by nature can attain the fullness of his being only when he lives in a polis: when he comes together with his fellows, whom he knows in person or by family or by reputation, to pursue the common good. Man is a political being because he is a personal being; and to be a person is, as I have said, to be oriented toward other persons. The individual is an abstraction. It is like sodium: it cannot be found isolated in nature. We can isolate sodium, artificially, as we can isolate persons, and we have done so, antisocially. To save man is to save men. It is not to save a Moses here and an Aaron there. It is to save the children of Israel.

Everywhere we go in the modern world, we encounter

a struggle between those who champion the individual in this sense and the collective in that, or the collective in this sense and the individual in that. It is a false struggle, or a struggle between falsehoods. The individual is less than a man, and the collective is made of creatures rendered less than men. The full human being is the person, and there is no personhood without being-for. You cannot have a human life as an individual or as a grain in a heap of sand. You can have it only in a society, whose bonds are those of friendship.

So when I hear people say that Jesus did not come among us to found a church, I must wonder what kind of Jesus they worship. It is a jelly Jesus, without bones. Think of the moment of Simon's confession. Jesus has asked the disciples who the people roundabout were saying that he was, and they said, "Some say that thou art John the Baptist: some, Elias; and others, Jeremias, or one of the prophets" (Mt 16:14). These Jews with their guesses were placing Jesus within the history of their people, a people with a long-established worship, with a year full of feasts that Jesus himself observed, and communal prayers that Jesus himself prayed. We can imagine no Greeks saying, "Some say thou art Cleisthenes the democrat, and others, Demosthenes the rhetor." But Jesus was more than those Jewish prophets or spokesmen. He was not one who pointed, but the one to whom they had pointed, for "your father Abraham rejoiced to see my day" (Jn 8:56). So when Simon finally responded, "Thou art the Christ, the Son of the living God", Jesus quite literally christened him, giving him a new name: "Thou art Peter, and upon this rock I will build my church; and the gates of hell shall not prevail against it" (Mt 16:18). Jesus came to save not only people but *peoples*: "Go ye therefore, and teach all nations, baptizing them in the name of the Father, and of the Son, and of the Holy Ghost" (Mt 28:19).

The Incarnation implies the Church. Why should all human enterprises be granted the virtue of organization, except the Church? When people say they do not believe in "organized religion", I ask myself why the same people believe in organized government, organized militaries, organized education, organized mass entertainment, organized bodies of every kind imaginable, but not organized religion. If a religion is not organized, it is not fully human. It is a fancy or a phantasm. It is not real. And maybe that is why some people demand that it be unorganized: they want to keep it from having any influence. But for the Son of God to come among us in the flesh makes no sense at all if he were soon to recede into a mere memory, to be cherished by a hobbyist or an antiquarian. It is as if Thomas were to place his hand in the side of a conjecture.

But "as the body is one, and hath many members, and all the members of that one body, being many, are one body: so also is Christ" (1 Cor 12:12). The members in the Church are bound together by charity, so that each member of the body does not lose its individuality but gains it all the more, "for the body is not one member, but many" (12:14). The dilemma of the singular and the plural is resolved in the Body of Christ, not by way of compromise, but by that charity that increases being by increasing love. Look at the painting of the Final Judgment by Fra Angelico, and you see saints together in wonder and rejoicing—not drab as are the crushed citizens in a collective, and not gloomily dispersed and lonely as are the half-formed grubs who take pride in their isolation, but bright, colorful, and each one himself and no other. For here too is a law of being: "Whosoever will save his life shall lose it: and whosoever will lose his life for my sake shall find it" (Mt 16:25).

In the city called Unreal, the more often people talk about community, the less likely you are to find a real one anywhere. Indeed, "community" often denotes no more than some shared taste or vice, as in "the ice-fishing community", or "the gay community", or "the Providence College community", or "the intelligence community"—communities without bodies, notional creatures that might better be called common anonymities, wherein hardly anybody knows anybody else, and hardly anybody shares anything important with anybody else. In Unreal, we chafe against threats to our individuality, when we are immersed in the mass phenomena and have hardly any individuality to be threatened. In Unreal, we march in mass protests to show our unity, when we have hardly anything real to be united: mere tastes, imagined grievances, flights of emotion, and the vapors. We cannot resolve the tension between what I want and what you want, and between what anyone may want and what the whole needs. Witness the multiplication of rights and the evaporation of duties. The Church holds the answer—though most of the time her prelates themselves do not understand it.

In the city called Unreal, there is a lot of chatter about the spirit of this and the spirit of that: the spirit of the American Constitution, the spirit or specter of Vatican II, school spirit, and so forth. It might be useful to replace "spirit" with "spit", as in what happened to the phrase "spirit and image", which became "spit and image" and then "spittin' image" and "spitting image". Almost all talk about "spirit" in our time is worth no more than spit. Maybe less, because spit does serve a real purpose: it keeps your mouth

and throat moist and helps you eat your food. Spirit in the
contemporary sense dries up everything in sight.

That is in part because of the spit of the egalitarian. Think
of the body again. There is no body without hierarchy. It
must be so. In the Body of Christ, with Christ as the head,
there must also be hierarchy, lest the body be but a notional
body, or the body of jelly Christ. For "Christ is the head of
the church: and he is the saviour of the body" (Eph 5:23),
and "we are members of his body, of his flesh, and of his
bones" (5:30), even "lively stones, [who] are built up a spiritual house, an holy priesthood, to offer up spiritual sacri-
fices, acceptable to God by Jesus Christ" (1 Pet 2:5).

That is all to the good, both naturally and supernatu-
rally. Naturally, in the world beyond the straitjacket of Unreal, you cannot get anything complicated or difficult accomplished without hierarchy. The Tigris and Euphrates
Rivers, prone to destructive floods, could be used for irrigation only by a most precise and far-extending system
of trenches and canals, especially since their grade within
the Mesopotamian plain is about one inch per mile. Read
that sentence over again. The hierarchies of Sumeria and
Babylon did not merely make the irrigation possible. In a
sense they *were* the irrigation: the complex system of master
builders, engineers, soldiers, foremen, and workers. You are
not going to span the Hudson River with egalitarians hold-
ing hands. There must be a plan and a chain of command.
In the stones and piers and arches themselves we find hierarchy. Otherwise the bridge falls. There is a name for a
body in which all the cells are equal. It is called a corpse,
and the cells are equally dead.

In Unreal, we pay for a fiction of equality of one sort
by establishing very real inequalities of other sorts. So we
pretend, in Unreal, that a female soldier on the battlefield

is going to be just as capable as a male soldier, when every single physical activity that can be measured and every single physical feature of their bodies and every testament of experience is against it. To do so, we must engage in massive self-deception, and put all the male soldiers under compulsion to deceive themselves and to suppress their natural desire to protect women. We must waste all kinds of resources in money and manpower and time just to bring the woman, temporarily and uneasily, up to the level of a rather poor example of the male, and ever afterward to try to keep her from slipping back. The inequality of political power that our betters must assume to make this happen is immense.

In the world that God made, and in the Church that Christ founded, we grow taller by bowing, as Chesterton said, and we long for the time when we will be individual persons indeed, each one of us a distinct and unrepeatable instantiation of the divine image, and each related to all the rest as members of one body—each one glorying in the gifts that God has given to others, thanking him not only that he gave to Michelangelo the gift of art but that he withheld the same gift from us that we might love it all the more in Michelangelo. For in the body, the foot does not jealously keep to itself its capacity to walk, nor the hand its capacity to grasp, and the foot is not envious of the hand or the hand of the foot, but hand is for foot and foot is for hand; as man is for woman and woman for man, most fully so when both man and woman are for God.

In the Church of the Real, the skies are filled with luminaries bright and dim, and not all of one color. It requires Unreality to give us grids instead.

God made us good, and we have fallen away from that good. We sin. We do so all the time. "In sin did my mother conceive me", says the psalmist (Ps 51:5). We are, says Augustine, *incurvatus* by sin, hunched over, prone to look earthward rather than to heaven.

The sins are real and unreal. They really are sins, and they lead us into unreality. At the empty heart of every sin there is that antiessential embrace of a lie. "Ye shall be as gods", said the serpent to Eve, when Adam and Eve had already been made in the image of God (Gen 3:5). Thus did he lie two ways, denying their divinity and the generosity of God, and promising that they could have divinity by their own will, or worse and sillier, by the instrumentality of a tree. Call it the first moment of technological arrogance.

The sins are real. If you stand on the ledge of a high building and step forward, the emptiness will not bear you up. If you harden your heart against God and your neighbor, you will collapse into a cold, hard lump of self. You will be Ebenezer Scrooge at best—for Scrooge at least obeyed the law and had an acidulous sense of humor. If you debauch yourself, you will riddle your body with weakness and perhaps a terrible disease, and your soul will be in a worse state still. But the sins are lies too. You say, "I may kill this child I have made, because he would only be unhappy if I allowed him to live", and besides, you are hardly paying for your rent as it is, and you might have to sell your car or take a year off from school. It is a lie, and you know it. But the more egregious the lie is, the more energy you expend in telling it, and if anybody should name the lie for what it is, you will turn on the truth teller with all the ferocity of a wounded and cornered animal.

In Unreal, the only sins are political; and therefore there is no forgiveness. There is plenty of intolerance: we are like people afflicted with the shingles from head to toe, so that the slightest touch, even a breeze that tickles the hair on our neck, will feel like burning fire. We must not be touched: hence the favorite Scripture in Unreal is, "Judge not, that ye be not judged" (Mt 7:1). Yet the citizens of Unreal do nothing but judge: their own relentless discomfort, their restlessness, their sins and their refusal to acknowledge that there is such a thing as sin, make them all the more intolerant when someone else causes them the slightest discomfort of body or mind or soul.

The citizens of Unreal who go to church services do not want to be forgiven their sins. They want to be spared that. Think of Augustine's hunchback. Habitual sin is a crippling thing. "Guai a voi, anime prave!" cries Dante's Charon to the souls gathered at the shore of the Acheron, awaiting the ferry that will herd them like sheep into hell: "Woe to you, crooked souls!"[5] The crooked souls need to be made straight by Christ, the healer. And how do we heal a leg that has been set wrong? We break it and set it right. Forgiveness is not a shrug and a thumbs-up.

"Heal me of my sin", prays the man who has grown tired of dodging and making excuses. He says it with trepidation, because he trusts that God will answer that prayer.

In the world outside of grace, when you forgive somebody, you mean that you will no longer think about what he has done, or you will not hold it against him. That is all. That is at the best. But the offender is still hunched over. We want the forgiveness granted by God, who can call up a universe out of nothing. God can raise a human soul from

---

[5] Dante, *Inferno*, canto 3, line 81.

the deadness of sin. He can change us utterly. He can make us finally into the real persons we were meant to be. He may proceed slowly with his salutary influences and inspiration, as with Malcolm Muggeridge, who took a long and meandering way from secular leftism to the faith, with many byways of sin in the meantime. He may strike Paul blind at a stroke. He may break open the heart of the thief gasping out his life on the cross beside Jesus. Forgiveness, one way or another, is dramatic, and it will hurt. But the healing is real. The salve of happy talk keeps the sore beneath from healing. The caustic of grace burns away the rot so that real flesh will take its place.

To ask for grace is to assume that you know that you need it. One of the inscriptions over the gate at the ancient temple of Delphi was simply this: "Know thyself." That was taken to be one of the most difficult tasks of a lover of wisdom. Think of Narcissus gazing into the pool, infatuated. We do not know ourselves. "I am a worm, and no man", said the psalmist (Ps 22:6). That was an exercise in self-knowledge. "I repent in dust and ashes", said Job. People who do not know themselves may ask why there is evil in the world. "Because God is giving you another chance" should be our reply. Mr. Crangle in Price Day's short story "Four O'Clock" will remedy the problem of evil in the world by turning every bad person into a dwarf when the clock strikes four. It does, and Mr. Crangle suddenly finds that he cannot reach high enough to give his pet parrot a nut.

In Unreal, the object of human life is to try to force reality, including human nature itself, to conform to your desires: this is what is called being true to yourself. You are to "follow your dreams", and when the rest of the world does not conform to them, you lash out in anger. I do not want to follow my dreams. They prove to be empty or to be nightmares of self-absorption. I pray for reality, and tremble, because that means that God will show me what I am. Atheists say that we invent a make-believe God. I say that it requires all the make-believe in the world for me to pretend that I do not need God; and I pray also that God, while he is yet making me real, will make believe that I am already a good and faithful servant—if it is not impious to imagine it of God.

## The Resurrection of the Body

In Unreal, we fling ourselves from one error to its converse. We scorn the flesh, and we live like libertines. The male body and the female body for us have no meaning. We are simultaneously obsessed with sex and numb to it. We go so far as to mutilate it in a vain quest for some evanescent sexual integrity. We are only-bodies and no-bodies at once.

The single thing that most puzzled the sophisticated audience on the Hill of Mars, when Saint Paul came to Athens to preach, was the resurrection of the flesh. Had Paul said that the spirit of Jesus had been raised to heaven, not one member of that audience would have been struck by it. Plato seemed to teach that the soul was immortal because it was immaterial, and that it was immaterial because it saw and reasoned about immaterial things. Hence the words above the gate to his Academy: "Let no one who is ignorant of geometry enter here." For geometry treats of things that are not material. They are what they are, they do not change, and our knowledge of them is true and irrefragable. The Epicureans believed that the soul was composed of exceedingly tenuous and slippery soul atoms, which would disperse through the breath and the pores of the body at death; but they were in the minority. The so-called mystery cults promised spiritual immortality to the devotees who had been let in on the secrets and who had undergone the amoral rites of purification.

The Resurrection of Jesus was nothing like any of it. Hence the stir on Mars Hill.

How can the Resurrection be? We might parry the question by affirming that nothing is impossible with God. We need not do so. I will attempt a few suggestions, not to say, "This is how it is so", but to show that a Christian *realism* brings us into the realm of enlightening possibilities rather than leaves us in the darkness of unreality posing as certainty.

Look at the child coloring with crayons a picture of a dog. What do your eyes see? Think carefully. Your eyes do not see a child, or the crayons, or a dog. Your eyes see only color, including black and white and gray. It is your *mind* that sees the child, the crayons, and the dog. The seeing is intellectual. If we go on to ask, "What is the child?", the materialist answer is reductive and strangely unreal. It is that the child is the matter that makes him up: the chemicals that compose his body. But what are those chemicals? They are arrangements of atomic particles—neutrons and protons and electrons—and subatomic particles. What are the neutrons and protons and electrons? What are they made up of? Quarks, in the case of neutrons and protons; but what are quarks? And why are they the same from place to place and time to time? Physicists such as Stephen Hawking suggest that there is no difference between the proton, let us say, and the mathematical equations that the proton obeys; they are the same. But that would resolve the entire universe into a bundle of math. What has happened to the child, the picture, and the dog? And what about those mathematical laws?

They too recede into darkness. People who do not dabble in mathematics may suppose that all equations are soluble in principle, whether or not we have gotten around to solving them. That is not true. There are countless equations that are insoluble: they never are going to be solved with exactitude. Nor are they always complicated. Draw a regular heptagon: a seven-sided figure with equal sides. Now make a diagonal, connecting one of the points with another. What is the length of that diagonal, compared with the length of the side? We can approximate the answer, but we do not know the exact ratio, and we never will; the problem is algebraically insoluble. If that is the case for a little heptagon, how much more must it be the case when we are talking about the innumerable interactions of billions and billions of neurons in a human brain?

We pretend to know what matter is capable of. We do not know. The possibilities are inexhaustible. We cannot say simultaneously that all is material and that the material is purely mathematical; we will have sawed off the limb of the tree we are sitting on. Christian realism returns thus to the primacy of things themselves: dogs, drawings, and children, and of the minds that perceive and understand and imagine things. We Christians reject the constitutional fallacy, which collapses things into the matter that happens, at a certain moment, to make them up. The materialist who denies that God exists, on the grounds that all is material, must deny that he himself exists, as an identifiable thing that lasts through time. Philosopher and scientist Daniel Dennett has done so, resolving the mysterious fact of consciousness by denying that we are conscious at all. Rather than go where an acknowledgment of consciousness will lead—namely, to the real existence of immaterial things and then to the possibility of the existence of God—he prefers to deny what we all experience, to call it an illusion. When your premises lead you to an absurd conclusion, it is time to reject the premises. If the premises of materialism lead us to conclude that we have no consciousness, and even that persons do not exist but are only mental constructs, then we must affirm that matter alone is insufficient to explain anything—woefully so.

Then there is the picture, the representation, of the dog. Such a drawing does not exist in nature. Only personal intention can produce it. It is a sign, an idea, communicated from person to person, from mind to mind, by the agency of the child who draws it and the crayon he uses. The mind not only sees the dog. It sees the representation of the dog; it sees the idea. "I have a picture", says the smarter-than-average Neanderthal in William Golding's *Inheritors* (1955).[6] He and the rest of his little family group are trying to cross a rushing stream. He thinks of throwing a fallen tree across it; he thinks of what he has never seen before. The mind sees what could be: and what could be but is not now cannot be resolved back into existent matter alone. Yes, the "picture" is also made manifest by the agency of activity in the brain, but that is no more than to say that my hand moves when I move my hand. And why do you make the picture at all? Because you see, in your childlike way, that the dog is good. In your human and creaturely mode you repeat the affirmation of God in the beginning, when he saw that the light was good.

Then why should we balk at the idea that God might raise us to new life in the flesh? The God who spangled the heavens with masses of energy and matter, in "measure and number and weight", as the author of Wisdom has it

[6] William Golding, *The Inheritors* (San Diego: Harvest Books, 1955), p. 15.

(11:20), can surely change the measure, the weight, and the numbers.

Or perhaps the numbers are already among us, and we are not aware of them.

The resurrection of the flesh—why not the raising of an $n$-dimensional reality to its fullness in $n+1$ dimensions? Where is the violation of law if you are brought out of the Flatland of this glorious universe into a greater universe, whereof Flatland was a projection? To a creature of limited vision, the working of ordinary objects in an ordinary space beyond his ken will strike him as miraculous, should they occasionally intersect with his own lesser space; that is the gist of the novel *Flatland* (1884), by Edwin Abbott, the Anglican minister with the mathematical imagination. Physicists say that the universe can have come about from a special kind of "nothing", a nothing that comes equipped with mathematical and physical laws, and latent quanta. That does not move us at all toward a solution of the question, why is there something and not nothing? If the physicist answers, "Because that is the way it is", we can reply, "Then nothing prevents the existence of a world transcending this one."

But we Christians should return always to matters of fact. Jesus rose from the dead. All attempts to explain away the event break upon the rocks of testimony, human nature, subsequent events, and the prophecies that foretold it. We have in addition the saints and their miracles, and most miraculous of all the very existence of men and women whose like the world had never known and does not know now, the transformation of the world itself by the Christian faith, and the unique artifact testifying to a unique person and a unique event, the Shroud of Turin. Sometimes, I know, people will hesitate, because the promise of resurrection seems too good. We do not deserve it. But the Church confesses that we do not deserve it. We did not deserve that there should be a world to begin with and that we should dwell in it. We did not deserve the goodness of dogs and children and pictures. The God who made the world from nothing can give us what he will. Let us not demur.

## Christ the Lord

And I return to Jesus, the anointed one of God.

People who flee from Jesus will say that he is a fiction. They must never have read much fiction. The saints try to live in imitation of Jesus. But Jesus is in imitation of no one. In some respects, Buddha is like Jesus, because both men drew disciples to themselves, and both set little store by the riches that most men pursue. But Jesus is not like Buddha. It would be more than a reduction to suggest as much. It would be a falsification. We may say that Moses was like Muhammad, as one fiery lawgiver is like another, despite all their differences. In that severely limited sense, Moses is like Jesus; but Jesus is not like Moses. David was king of the Jews, as is Jesus; but Jesus is not like David. "My kingdom is not of this world", says Jesus (Jn 18.36). He might as well say that his kingship is like none other, although every king in this world, from the mild to the severe, from a Saint Louis IX to an Ivan the Terrible, is somehow a distant or distorted reflection of him.

People who flee from Jesus will say that his sayings were made up by the evangelists and are a fiction. These people must never have attempted to write fiction. Those who heard Jesus were astonished, because "he taught them as one that had authority, and not as the scribes" (Mk 1:22). I teach as a scribe, referring to scribes before me. The psalmist did so also: "My tongue is the pen of a ready writer" (Ps 45:1). Try, careless scoffer, try to pen a parable within a thousand miles of one of the parables of Jesus. I will even permit you to imitate them. It has been two thousand years now, and who has done so? The sayings of Saint Francis may be humorous and delightful and keen, but by comparison with the sayings of Jesus they are like the sprightly drawings of a child as compared with the work of Michelangelo—or with the work of some unknown artist who makes Michelangelo look like a child. One way we can tell the falseness of the so-called gnostic gospels is that they turn Jesus into a dullard and a muddler; they give us a Jesus that prideful and religion-besotted people might imagine.

Chesterton as usual expresses the matter far better than I can. Here, from *The Everlasting Man*:

> The morality of most moralists ancient and modern, has been one solid and polished cataract of platitudes flowing for ever and ever. That would certainly not be the impression of the imaginary independent outsider studying the New Testament. He would be conscious of nothing so commonplace and in a sense of nothing so continuous as that stream. He would find a number of strange claims that might sound like the claim to be the brother of the sun and moon; a number of very startling pieces of advice; a number of stunning rebukes; a number of strangely beautiful stories. He would see some very gigantesque figures of speech about the impossibility of threading a needle with a camel or the possibility of throwing a mountain into the sea. He would see a number of very daring simplifications of the difficulties of life; like the advice to shine upon everybody indifferently as does the sunshine or not to worry about the future any more than the birds. He would find on the other hand some passages of almost impenetrable darkness, so far as he is concerned, such as

the moral of the parable of the Unjust Steward. Some of
these things might strike him as fables and some as truths;
but none as truisms.[7]

No truisms, and especially not truisms that are false. Think
of a human mind given nothing to feed upon but what you
could put upon a bumper sticker. Make peace, not war. Co-
exist. If you think education is expensive, try ignorance.
Every child a wanted child. Make America great again. Support our troops. Think globally, act locally. And so forth, to
produce nations full of people with intellectual and spiritual
rickets, whose legs will snap like toothpicks.

But Jesus leads us where the verdant pastures grow. He is
the Good Shepherd, and that means that there is good feeding where he goes. We can never come to the end of understanding his words, his deeds, his person: wisdom clears
the way for wisdom, as we in our happy sense of ignorance
go ever further into the truth. We might very well take his
words almost at random, as a child picking up conch shells
on the shore and wondering at their mysterious shapes and
colors. "Ye have heard that it hath been said, An eye for an
eye, and a tooth for a tooth: But I say unto you, That ye resist
not evil: but whosoever shall smite thee on thy right cheek,
turn to him the other also" (Mt 5:38–39). Who among us in
Unreal, especially in our character as political agents, will not
rejoice when our enemies give us cause, or but the shadow
of a cause, to punish them? But what great and sweet life
might be ours, if we could set vengeance aside, and pride,
and do as Jesus commands!

"Ye cannot serve God and mammon", says Jesus (Mt
6:24), and is that not true? "For where your treasure is,

[7] G.K. Chesterton, *The Everlasting Man*, in *The Collected Works of G.K. Chesterton*, vol. 2 (San Francisco: Ignatius Press, 1986), pp. 322–23.

there will your heart be also" (6:21). Think. Who is the God to which Jesus would direct our hearts? He is the one from whom all blessings flow, who has clothed the lilies of the field in raiment more lovely than Solomon in all his glory ever wore, to whom we owe our very existence. To serve mammon then is to behave as if we could by taking care about it add a cubit to our stature (6:27). The attempt is vain, for, says the Preacher, "What profit hath a man of all his labour which he taketh under the sun?" (Eccl 1:3). We scramble on a treadmill. Shakespeare:

> If thou art rich, thou'rt poor.
> For, like an ass whose back with ingots bows,
> Thou bear'st thy heavy riches but a journey,
> And death unloads thee.[8]

We step off that treadmill and walk the way of trust in God. For are we not bound by the false god of self-sufficiency? Do the chains not chafe the wrists and ankles? Or perhaps I am mistaken, and a walk in an airport is like going to gather mayflowers, and Wall Street is a carnival of hilarity.

"Except ye be converted, and become as little children," says Jesus, "ye shall not enter into the kingdom of heaven" (Mt 18:3). That is reality again. Children are open to the universe. They do not stand on their own power. They can receive. The child looks upon Jesus and says, "I want to be with him." Everywhere else in the world, the child is but a grub, a larva. He is valued by what he will be or will earn when he grows up. If that is not much, he may be dispensed with, as the ancient pagans exposed defective children, giving them back to the gods, as the conscience-oiling euphemism had it then; or he may be pulled apart to bits, for

---

[8] William Shakespeare, *Measure for Measure*, ed. Jonathan Crewe (New York: Penguin Books, 2017), act 3, scene 1, lines 25–28.

he is no more than a "choice", as the conscience-cauterizing evasion has it now. Christ alone not only invites us to become children but warns us against that slow growth that leads to spiritual ossification and death.

"Ye blind guides," Jesus cries out against the moralists of his time, "which strain at a gnat, and swallow a camel" (Mt 23:24). We all do that. It is remarkable, how easily those camels go down the gullet, while we gag on gnats. It is all an exercise in unreality. A man with roaming hands touches a woman's shoulder when she finds it uncomfortable, and that offense—and it really is an offense—might end his career; but fornication, no big deal. A woman lets her children play in the back street where she lives, just as children in towns have always done, and her meddlesome neighbor calls the police; but the same neighbor gives a smile at the instructions in perversion that the child will receive at school. Use the wrong adjective or pronoun, and your career will be in danger, but if you spit out profanities and obscenities against the proper targets, you will be congratulated as a regular artist of words. We are actors in our own plays, casting ourselves as the heroes and everybody else as villains. Jesus comes to tell us otherwise.

When many of his disciples abandoned him, because he gave them too much reality, Jesus turned to the apostles and asked if they would leave him too. "To whom shall we go?" said Peter. "Thou hast the words of eternal life" (Jn 6:68). But there is more, always more. Other wise men give us words, though they are but shadows of the words that Jesus gives us. Jesus gives us what surpasses words as the greatest does the least. He gives us the Word, himself. "He that eateth my flesh, and drinketh my blood, dwelleth in me, and I in him" (Jn 6:56). It is not metaphorical. Jesus and his audience knew about metaphors. They were waiting for him to give them a sign that he did not mean to be taken in that full fleshly way. He refused.

At a stroke, Jesus gives us what is more humbly real than our bread and wine, and more exalted than our highest conceptions of deity; it is "immensity cloistered in thy dear womb", as John Donne says of the Virgin Mary,[9] or the kingdom of God in a mustard seed. I think of that Blessed Sacrament, and there is no infinitesimal portion of the material universe that does not gleam with the possibility of glory, and there is no infinitude of divinity that God cannot house within the walls of the material: a womb, a manger, a man praying in the desert, a man suffering upon a cross, a body laid in a tomb, a Savior risen in glory; a mustard seed, a thought, an impulse of the will, to turn and be converted and be real.

---

[9] John Donne, "Nativity", line 1.